Real People

**Amish and Mennonites in
Lancaster County, Pennsylvania**

Fourth Edition

A. Martha Denlinger

HERALD PRESS
Scottdale, Pennsylvania
Waterloo, Ontario

Library of Congress Cataloging-in-Publication Data
Stahl, Martha Denlinger, 1931-
    Real people : Amish and Mennonites in Lancaster County,
    Pennsylvania / A. Martha Denlinger, — 4th ed.
        p. cm.
    Includes bibliographical references and index.
    ISBN 0-8361-3616-0
        1. Mennonites—Pennsylvania—Lancaster County. 2. Amish—
Pennsylvania—Lancaster County. 3. Lancaster County (Pa.)—Social
life and customs. I. Title.
    F157.L2S72 1993
    974.8'15—dc20
                                                        92-26887
                                                        CIP

The paper used in this publication is recycled and meets the minimum
requirements of American National Standard for Information
Sciences—Permanence of Paper for Printed Library Materials, ANSI
Z39.48-1984.

Except as otherwise indicated, Scripture quotations are from the *Holy Bible: New
International Version*; copyright © 1973, 1978, 1984 by the International Bible Soci-
ety, and used by permission of Zondervan Publishers. Texts marked NRSV are
from the *New Revised Standard Version Bible*, copyright 1989, by the Division of
Christian Education of the National Council of the Churches of Christ in the
USA, and are used by permission. Those marked KJV are from the *King James
Version of the Holy Bible*.

PHOTO CREDITS: *William Albert Allard, front cover; Jonathan Charles, 13, 24, 30,
39, 44, 54; Fern Clemmer, 51; Eastern Mennonite Board of Missions and Charities, top of
80; EMBMC photo by Dale Gehman, bottom of 80; Jerry Irwin, 61; MCC photo by
Lowell Detweiler, 64; Everett Newswanger, 17, 27, 38, 49, 57; Joe Tritsch, 10, 33.*

REAL PEOPLE
Copyright © 1975, 1981, 1986, 1993 by Herald Press,
    Scottdale, Pa. 15683. Published simultaneously in Canada by
    Herald Press, Waterloo, Ont. N2L 6H7. All rights reserved
International Standard Book Number: 0-8361-3616-0
Printed in the United States of America
Book design by Gwen Stamm

01 00 99 98 97 96 95 94 93 20 19 18 17 16 15 14 13 12
105,000 copies of all editions in print

To
the late Emory and Ruth Herr,
two of the important *Real People* in my life,
this book is gratefully dedicated.

Preface

This book attempts to answer questions tourists ask about the Amish and Mennonites in Lancaster County, Pennsylvania. It developed out of my interaction with hundreds of sincerely interested people at the Mennonite Information Center, where I have worked part-time since 1967.

During the summer of 1968, Mennonite history professor Grant Stoltzfus gave a series of illustrated lectures at the Center. A question-and-answer period followed each presentation. The staff recorded, compiled, and categorized the inquiries. The answers to these questions became the basis of my text. I have added information which I feel is pertinent and interesting.

My treatment of the subject is primarily regional. It is not intended to be a history or a textbook on theology, but simply to tell you about my people, the Mennonites, and my neighbors, the Amish. We truly are *Real People.*

Appreciation goes out to all who have encouraged me in this project. I am grateful to the past and present staff of Mennonite Information Center, to the Eastern Mennonite Board of Missions and Charities, and the Mennonite Historical Library for assisting me in compiling information. I also thank the numerous persons who gave me valuable assistance in personal interviews. The Lancaster Christian Writers' Fellowship and the St. Davids Christian Writers' Conference deserve much credit for inspiring me to write and for offering valuable hints along the way.

I am deeply indebted to the Mennonite Church, of which I am happy to be a member, and to the Strasburg congregation in particular. I recognize my mother's devotion to a simple life and to the Mennonite Church. I also thank her for her willingness to assume household chores so that I could pursue the writing of this book.

I have tried to be accurate and objective in my presentation.

However, my own convictions and opinions will undoubtedly come through. I trust that the reader will not only become informed about the Amish and Mennonites, but also grow to appreciate the faith that gives purpose and meaning to their lives.

—A. Martha Denlinger

Preface to the 1981 Edition

The Amish and Mennonite community in Lancaster County continues to grow and change. The basic distinctions discussed in *Real People* are still true. However, some of the statistics have been updated. I have also rewritten much of chapter 12. I am grateful to the publisher for granting me the privilege of a minor revision as the book goes into its fifth printing.

—A. Martha Denlinger Stahl

Preface to the 1986 Edition

As I researched and reviewed *Real People* for this revision, I found that the bulk of the material remains relevant and correct. However, statistics keep changing. This update also reflects changes in practice, gives new information, and contains many new photographs.

I wish to express my thanks to Paul M. Schrock, Herald Press editor, for his alertness and careful timing in keeping *Real People* current. This third edition comes at a time when many people—some curious and others seriously searching—are reaching out for information about the Amish and the Mennonites.

—A. Martha Denlinger Stahl

Preface to the 1993 Edition

My publisher tells me there are now 100,000 copies of *Real People* in print. I am delighted with this report and want to continue to share accurate information; hence, the need again to update my writing.

I wrote this revision of *Real People* while living in Germany. I am grateful to my colleagues from near and far who sent me the information I requested. My special thanks goes to Maribel Kraybill, director of Mennonite Information Center in Lancaster, Pa., for her prompt and detailed answers to my questions.

—A. Martha Denlinger Stahl
Lancaster, Pennsylvania

Foreword

In the past thirty-five years, a tourist attraction has come into its own that draws 3 1/2 to 5 million persons annually, not only from the Eastern megalopolis of the United States, but also from the Midwest, the South, the Far West, and foreign countries. This attraction is the fertile Amish countryside that fans eastward in a triangle from Lancaster City in southeastern Pennsylvania.

Here the tourist can personally observe a kind of "archaeological find," to use a sociologist's term in referring to the Amish people and their somewhat medieval culture. First transplanted from Germany's Rhineland to Pennsylvania in the early 1700s, these people have become (sometimes reluctantly and never completely) a part of American pluralistic society. They are found in over twelve states.

Tourists who cruise over the network of macadam roads that interlace the Amish countryside may have to drive behind a horse-drawn buggy. They should slow the pace, gaze on the green fields, and purchase some fruit or vegetables from a roadside stand. If possible they should request an expert guide to conduct them over the area and learn firsthand of the language, attire, folkways, music, and family life of one of America's important minority groups.

A. Martha Denlinger's description in *Real People* stands in a long and worthy tradition of authentic and sympathetic treatments of this socioreligious group. In October 1869, the *Atlantic Monthly* carried Phebe Earl Gibbon's discerning article on her Amish neighbors among whom she lived as a Quaker for twenty years, noting their virtues and shortcomings with much accuracy. In 1942 the United States Department of Agriculture, impressed by the Amish stability and survival through the Depression, published a major study by Walter M. Kollmorgen on the Lancaster County Amish that found its way into major socio-logical works.

After living as the "quiet in the land" for over two centuries, the Amish were discovered by the world of theater. Broadway found a favorite American theatrical theme—the rural-urban contrast and conflict. *Plain and Fancy,* which ran on Broadway for several years, introduced the Eastern urbanite to another world near his door. Although Bird in Hand is only a few hours from Manhattan, it is centuries distant in values and social system.

Drawing from many years as a public school teacher in this area, A. Martha Denlinger, a native of Lancaster County, has mingled with thousands of tourists and listened to their comments. In *Real People* she shares the answers to common questions from her store of firsthand knowledge. She writes from the Mennonite point of view and carefully explains the similarities and differences between Amish and Mennonites.

Whether the Amish people and their culture will survive the tourism they have created is not an idle question. They are unlike the restoration of Colonial Williamsburg in Virginia and the reproduction of Old Sturbridge Village in Massachusetts. In contrast, here is an authentic description of a way of life that, even in modern times, transports us all into the living past.

—*The late Grant M. Stoltzfus*
Professor of Church History
Eastern Mennonite College
Harrisonburg, Virginia

Contents

The Old Order Amish have retained a strict way of life and emphasize close family relationships.

1

The Difference Between Amish and Mennonites

A recent visitor to Lancaster County concluded that the tourist bureau was paying people to dress like Amish and ride around in horse-drawn buggies until after Labor Day for the benefit of the tourists. This assumption is far from the truth. These people are *real.* They live here beside Mennonites and other neighbors. The productive soil of Lancaster County is a prime factor in the economy of both Amish and Mennonites. Their way of life springs from deep religious conviction together with a cultural carryover from Europe and is in no way intended for display.

The rural environment of an agricultural setting fulfills the desire of Amish and Mennonites to live and rear children in an atmosphere conducive to a wholesome life, separate from evil worldly influences.

Interested tourists frequently ask, "What is the difference between the Amish and the Mennonites?" Even many people who live in the county do not know what Mennonites and Amish believe. This chapter attempts to clarify the relation of these people to each other and point out their most obvious differences. You will need to proceed through the entire book, however, to get a detailed breakdown of likenesses and differences in beliefs and practices.

The Amish make up a part of the larger group known as Mennonites. They represent a "breakaway," although it might be equally correct to say that they began as a result of a strong conviction to continue some practices which the Mennonites were dropping. At the time of division, Amish and Mennonites appeared identical and held to the same biblical faith. The practice of shunning those excommunicated from the church created the main point of contention. Disagreement on minor issues also contributed to a decision to part ways in 1693.

The Amish today and their less conservative neighbors, the Mennonites, often live and work together in the community. But they worship separately. Both attempt to follow New Testament standards for living. They teach the entire Bible and believe that the New Testament is the fulfillment of the Old. They differ mainly in the interpretation of scriptural principles for practical matters of living.

The Jewish religion offers a corresponding breakdown into Ultra Orthodox, Orthodox, Conservative, and Reformed subgroups. A basic similarity exists between Amish and Mennonites. The difference depends largely on the degree to which the group has accommodated itself to the world around it.

The Old Order Amish have retained the strict way of life which includes a plain garb. The women wear long dresses of solid-colored material, black hose and shoes, a prayer veiling of white organdy material, and a black bonnet over the veiling when outer protection is appropriate. The men wear solid-colored shirts, dark broadfall trousers, and black felt or straw broadbrimmed hats. Adult men let their beards grow. The children dress much the same as the adults. In their homes the Amish speak Pennsylvania Dutch. Most Old Order Amish live on farms with no electricity, depend on horses to work their fields, and travel by horse and buggy. Members hold worship services

Mennonites generally dress less conservatively than Amish, own and use modern conveniences, and are interested in higher education.

in their homes where leaders read the German Bible and then preach in Pennsylvania Dutch. Amish oppose education above the eighth grade. No organized program of missions exists.

In contrast, the Mennonites generally own and use modern conveniences and are interested in higher education. They dress in a conservative manner but not always in a distinctive garb. They hold public worship in meetinghouses. Sunday schools, evening meetings, vacation Bible schools, and involvement in evangelism and missions are a part of Mennonite Church life. Wide variation exists among Mennonites, making it difficult to list specific Mennonite practices. The Amish demonstrate a more uniform way of life.

This brief comparison refers to the two largest bodies of plain people in the county, the Old Order Amish and the Lancaster Conference of the Mennonite Church. The main part of this book deals with these two bodies.

A number of other smaller but significant groups of Mennonites and Amish live in Lancaster. The Beachy Amish, as well as New Order Amish, and several conferences of Mennonites help complete the local scene. A later chapter will introduce these and note some religious groups and denominations which are historically related. The chapter will also attempt to clarify notions about those mistakenly thought to have some connection with Mennonites or Amish.

To report on the number of Amish and Mennonites presents a problem because these people traditionally shy away from counting members. Amish base this reluctance on two facts. First, the New Testament does not give figures on church membership. Second, in the Old Testament, David numbered the children of Israel, and that brought sorrow.

Therefore, any figures are estimates at best. Amish in Lancaster County's one hundred districts number approximately 16,000—a conservative count. Slightly less than half this number are baptized members. The total population of the Amish community probably exceeds 130,000. This includes those living in the United States as well as in Canada.

The Lancaster Conference of the Mennonite Church numbers more than 18,500 baptized members. About 12,000 of these live in the county. The total population of all groups of Mennonites in the United States and Canada is approximately 380,500 members plus unbaptized children. Over 476,000 additional Mennonites plus children live in other countries of the world. There are approximately 856,600 baptized members in all groups of Mennonites worldwide. The total Mennonite world community including children is estimated to be over 1,367,000 persons.

2

The
Impact
of Tourism

An aggressive young woman drove up to a country store in her sporty convertible. Seeing an Amishman, she hurriedly jumped out with a camera and asked if she could take his picture. The Amishman, noting her brief red shorts, quipped, "I don't know what you'd want with my picture. I don't think I look any worse than you do." The surprised tourist quickly got into her sports car and drove off.

Amish often turn their backs to cameras. They take no pictures themselves and do not appreciate anyone photographing them. They base this objection on the second commandment, "Thou shalt not make unto thee any graven image, or any likeness of any thing that is in heaven above, or that is in the earth beneath, or that it in the water under the earth" (Exodus 20:4, KJV).

Most tourists come to Lancaster to see the Amish despite the

Tourists expect to observe the plain people in a quiet country setting. This is difficult because of increasing commercialization and the vast number of people who visit Lancaster County each summer.

ever-increasing number of tourist attractions. The Amish person in a carriage rides sedately along, often forcing the slowing of five or ten cars behind the rig in a no-passing zone. The Amish may take the attitude, "Well, that's what you've come to see. Look at us." Others will move over and let the line pass. Their politeness is not always rewarded, however. One Amishman relates that twice he pulled over, as he often does, only to have the tourist pass and then quickly stop up ahead and shoot pictures of him driving along. This, of course, is much to his dislike.

Reaction to tourism varies, as do tourists. Many tourists respect the Amish and do not intentionally cause offense. If they are fortunate enough to become acquainted with Amish people, they enjoy them and find them indeed to be *Real People.*

The Amish appear to discipline themselves and obviously take the tourism better than many non-Amish residents. They learn to ignore or endure the insults and the gazing while they continue stable in their unique way of life.

Non-Amish who live in Bird in Hand, Intercourse, Paradise, and Strasburg are likely more annoyed by tourism than are the Amish. There are long lines of slow-moving buses and out-of-state cars, and this tests the patience of local persons as they drive to and from work by car. Many also empathize with their Amish neighbors and feel that tourism unfairly exploits them.

Of course, another faction of the population welcomes the tourist with open arms and hopes no recession or energy crisis will keep them away. These operate the various tourist attractions, motels, and restaurants.

How did it all begin? A Lancaster hotel's tours of Amish country probably stand as the earliest commercial venture. A museum farm and house opened in 1955, luring city folks to come and see how the Amish live. The production of a play about the Amish had its influence, and more recently a Hollywood film "invited" onlookers. Leading magazines have published articles about the Amish. Tourism has mushroomed! It continues to grow until the county can scarcely handle all the people who come to see the Amish, a people who do not wish to be on display.

Mennonites show mixed reactions, too. Some would probably like to say, "Tourists, go home!" Others benefit financially and enjoy meeting and talking with travelers from distant places.

Mennonites find another reason to become involved with tourists. For many years they have sent missionaries to the cities and to foreign countries. In 1958 a well-known Mennonite evangelist visited Lancaster, noted what was happening, and challenged a small group of Mennonites to rally to the opportunity to present the true meaning of the faith and practice to tourists. "Now they are coming to us instead of us needing to go to them," he pointed out. Around that same time, a local Mennonite couple saw the open door and had already begun a witness. Some leaders approached the Mission Board, which then accepted the call to administer a Mennonite Information Center.

Beginning in August 1958, the First Deaf Mennonite Church housed the initial activity of the Mennonite Information Center. Attendants gave directions and other routine tourist information, but deliberately led the discussion into more serious topics.

From that small beginning to the present Center operation at 2209 Millstream Road, many sincere seekers have been helped to see beneath the veneer of commercial tourism. In a recent year, approximately 60,000 people visited the Center. Many of these watched the 22-minute documentary film, *A Morning Song*. Mennonites from the Center guided over 2,000 tours, mostly in private cars, telling the authentic story of the Amish and Mennonites.

Tourists as well as local people wonder where all the commercialization will lead. Will the Amish move away? An elderly man interviewed by the writer says they will not move.

A Mennonite farmer says the tax structure presents a greater threat than tourism. If building developments continue to consume the good farmland, the tax structure to educate the children in these new homes will become exorbitant for the farmers that remain. The government taxes the whole farm just like they tax a person for the house where he raises his family. The farmhouse contains a comparable number of children to that of any other house. But the farmer pays school tax on his whole farm. The farmer is not demanding the frills in education. The ones who move into the new houses ask for expanded sports programs and elaborate facilities.

On the plus side, tourism brings a lot of money into the area, and the farmers don't have to pay taxes to educate the tourists' children. Consequently, tourists won't drive the Amish out as fast as the commercial and residential buildup with its threatening tax structure.

Tourists themselves, however, express chagrin at the increasing commercialization of the Amish. They want to see the plain people in a quiet country setting, eat Pennsylvania Dutch food in a small "noncommercial" restaurant, view farming operations on a real working farm, see livestock, and shop in the farmers' markets. They want to be directed away from the commercial tourist attractions. That kind of wishful thinking might well be realized if tourists numbered only several hundred people a month. But millions per year hope to realize the same kind of experience! Even if that elusive "quaint little village where we can see how the people really live" did exist, it would no longer be able to retain its serenity. With crowds of curious onlookers, how could it remain quaint and quiet?

What eludes many tourists is the fact that the Amish territory is not all so placid nor is it completely immune to the devastating forces of social change. Silently and covertly the battle goes on between those who want to commercialize the region even more and those who want to keep the farmlands intact. It should be noted that the word *Amish* in the name of any tourist attraction, motel, restaurant, movie, or other commercial venture indicates that the Amish do not own the establishment. They do not use the name of their religious denomination to advertise their businesses.

The serious question remains: Will tourism kill the culture that created it? To date the Amish on the whole remain steadfast. Only the future holds the answer as to how long they will continue to cope with the various pressures and conflicts moving in upon them. The majority of people, both non-Amish residents and tourists, would consider it a sad day if the Amish succumbed to these pressures and no longer retained their identity.

3

Home
and
Family

The glow of a large coal stove filled the room with a welcome warmth as I stepped inside on a cold day to wait while my Amish neighbor counted out three dozen eggs for me. As I sat down to chat a bit, I felt more than the physical warmth. The spotless kitchen, the noticeable absence of blaring radio or television, and the children sitting quietly at the long table with books, crayons, or games—these all created an atmosphere of healing to my weary mind. An Amish home is truly beautiful in its simplicity and peaceful in its separation from the world.

A Separate People

All the things that may appear odd to an onlooker stem from genuine convictions in relation to the importance of faith, farm, and family. These topics are discussed in later chapters. Yet all three come into focus as one considers the home.

The Scriptures command, "Do not conform any longer to the pattern of this world" (Romans 12:2), "Come out from them and be separate" (2 Corinthians 6:17), and "Do not love the world or the things in the world. The love of the Father is not in those who love the world" (1 John 2:15, NRSV). These and other Scriptures speak to the Amish of a distinctively different way of life. Exactly how they decide where to draw the line puzzles many people. Why gas and not electricity? Why bright colors but no printed dress fabrics? Why ride in cars but not own them? These and similar questions about their way of living are not easily answered.

In addition to the scriptural teaching on separation, the people show a strong reluctance to change. Once the church decides about a particular innovation, a strict adherence follows.

Modern Conveniences

Take the matter of electricity. Amish may have gas refrigerators and stoves, and gas or diesel engines for some farm operations (such as milking machines). But electricity is forbidden. The fourth commandment provided a reason for this when electricity first came into common use here. Amish did not want to make anyone work for them on Sunday. Most people feel that electricity is indispensable in the modern world. Nevertheless, Amish families thrive well without it. Kerosene lamps and gas lanterns provide light. Gas appliances, treadle sewing machines, waterwheels, and windmills are quite satisfactory. On the other hand, Mennonites generally do use electricity.

Radio and television are not accepted by Amish. Mennonites did not condone radio and television at first, and many Mennonites still oppose television. A smaller number do not have radios. Many Amish and Mennonite families get news from a daily newspaper, usually the *Intelligencer-Journal,* published by Lancaster Newspapers, but some families get no daily paper. A weekly paper, *The Budget,* published in Sugarcreek, Ohio, features news from scattered Amish settlements. Personal items help keep close ties among friends and relatives from distant points—such as who had what operation, who traveled where, who moved, as well as births, weddings, and deaths. A local Amish publication, *The Diary*, also carries significant news items for the Amish. It is compiled and published monthly as directed by a group of ministers and brothers of the church and printed by the Gordonville (Pennsylvania) Print Shop.

The common use of the automobile early in this century brought more decisions for the Amish and Mennonites. Cars enabled folks to get away from home and out into worldly influence with greater ease than was possible with horse-drawn carriages. Class distinction, indicating one's level of wealth, became more obvious among those who owned the various kinds of cars. The similarity of all Amish carriages allows little for status, but speaks of members all being equal. For whatever reasons, the Amish decided "no cars." Thereafter, for a member to own a car is an offense that results in excommunication. Mennonites, at first slow to change, later owned cars as an accepted convenience.

Health and Medicine

Rural living and a well-balanced diet contribute to the good health of Mennonite and Amish families. Illnesses and accidents, however, do occur and necessitate the services of doctors and hospitals. Amish, particularly, depend a great deal on home remedies, but they do go to doctors and receive hospital care. In general, no religious scruples prevent taking medicine and following doctors' orders.

A number of Mennonite doctors serve in Lancaster County. They do not limit their practice to their own people, nor do Mennonites go only to Mennonite doctors. The main hospitals in the county serve Amish and Mennonites along with other residents. The one Mennonite-operated hospital, Philhaven, located across the border in Lebanon County, provides excellent care and treatment for people suffering with mental problems. Mennonites and Amish, however, make up only a small percentage of the patients treated there.

Strong and stable family life is of great importance both to Mennonites and Amish. Four generations of Mennonites (above) work together on the farm.

Simple Houses

The interior of an Amish house is simple in decor. Blue, green, or gray walls; green window blinds; rag carpet strips and linoleum—these combine with neatness and cleanliness to create an atmosphere of serenity and comfort.

The Amish heat their homes with space heaters fueled by coal, gas, or oil. Heat does not reach all rooms. A heated kitchen provides a cozy setting for most of the family's activities. The parents usually sleep in a first-floor bedroom which has some heat. A small baby will sleep in the same room. Older children sleep upstairs and keep warm under blankets, beautiful homemade quilts, and comforters.

In contrast, Mennonite homes run the gamut from simplicity to luxury. Traditionally, Mennonites upheld "the simple life" (whatever that elusive phrase might include), but many have assimilated the lifestyle of the surrounding community.

Dialect

The use of the Pennsylvania Dutch dialect in the Amish home is another way of keeping apart from the world. Children speak Pennsylvania Dutch first. They learn English as they meet non-Amish people and study English in school. Adults continue to speak the dialect, even in the presence of non-Amish, in stores, markets, and on buses.

The dialect has nothing to do with the Dutch language spoken in Holland, nor does the so-called Pennsylvania Dutch culture in Lancaster County have any relationship to the culture of The Netherlands. It is really Pennsylvania German. *Dutch* is a misnomer from the German word *Deutsch* (German). The dialect is a combination of Palatinate German and English.

Youth

Problems with youth give Mennonite as well as Amish parents anxious days and sleepless nights. The children of these *Real People* don't all behave in saintly perfection. Youth experience temptations, doubts, and rebellious attitudes. Mennonites and more so-called liberal groups, however, lose a larger percentage of their youth than do Amish. Strange as it may seem, in spite of the strict life imposed upon them, Amish youth usually choose to remain Amish. A small percentage leave to unite with less plain churches. A strong family and group loyalty binds them together. Youth generally believe what their elders teach them, and the prospect of being placed under the ban compels them to consider the consequences seriously before they decide to leave.

The strong and stable family life is of great importance. For rural families, numerous farm and household chores provide a variety of activities in which family members work together. On the farm a mother of young children is always there lending a security missed by children of working mothers. Father, too, is usually on hand and can work with his sons. Fun combines with work, and play comes after work. Clubs, church functions, and committee meetings, especially for the Amish, do not compete with family solidarity by demanding several evenings a week. Evening provides a time to relax, play, sew fancywork, draw, knit, or read, depending upon the age and interest of each family member.

Amish usually have large families. Children are wanted, well cared for, and accepted as "a heritage from the Lord" (Psalm 127:3). The children are taught to work, thus becoming an economic asset. Not all families live on farms, but the farm or at least a rural home is considered most desirable.

Many Mennonites still believe the farm to be the ideal place to bring up their children. While historically a rural farm people, they have become increasingly urbanized.

Roles of Men and Women

The Amish emphasize the respective roles of men and women and uphold the biblical principle of sex distinction. Deuteronomy 22:5 says, "A woman must not wear men's clothing, nor a man wear women's clothing, for the Lord your God detests anyone who does this." Man takes his place in church leadership and as the head of the home. Woman complements man in her feminine role.

Amish houses are built to accommodate large families. When parents retire, a married son or daughter takes over the farm, adding a unit to the house for the older folks with separate kitchen, living room, and bedroom.

The role of Mennonite women cannot be so easily defined. Many Mennonite couples share household and child-rearing responsibilities and allow more flexibility in women's lives. A growing number work at least part-time outside the home, and many become educated beyond high school. Mennonite women may enter such professions as nursing, teaching, social work, writing, and speaking. Some are in business. Mennonite women also serve in the church as licensed deaconesses and as hospital chaplains.

The Elderly

The family scene is not complete without reference to the elderly. The younger people treat their elders with respect and consider it honorable to grow old. Seldom do Amish take residence in institutions for the aged. They work hard to rear their children; when they become old, their children take care of them. Their houses usually accommodate large families. But in addition, many houses include a separate unit with kitchen, living room, and bedroom. There the parents retire when a married son or daughter takes over the farm and the other children have married and live elsewhere. This addition to the building is often referred to as the granddaddy house.

It is not uncommon for Mennonite parents to live with a married son or daughter. However, Mennonites operate several high-quality institutions for the aged. Many prefer these homes above living with the younger generation. The noise and changing values of the children and grandchildren sometimes create problems for the elderly folks.

4

Manner of Dress

Five Mennonite girls wearing modest attire and their distinctive head covering attracted quite a bit of attention as they walked the streets in a New Jersey city. "Are you the 1 Corinthians 11 people?" asked an elderly gentleman. The girls found this a welcome opportunity to enter into a discussion about what they represent. The man did know the right Scripture for the head covering, but the girls were amused by this new label.

Mennonite and Amish people are conscious of the biblical admonitions that a woman's "beauty should not come from outward adornment, such as braided hair and the wearing of gold jewelry and fine clothes. Instead, it should be that of your inner self, the unfading beauty of a gentle and quiet spirit, which is of great worth in God's sight" (1 Peter 3:3-4). "Do not conform any longer to the pattern of this world, but be transformed by the renewing of your mind. Then you will be able to test and approve

Mennonites believe in simplicity and modesty in attire but generally do not wear a distinctive garb as do the Amish.

what God's will is—his good, pleasing and perfect will" (Romans 12:2). They use these and other scriptural teachings to decide how they should dress. The Mennonites allow more room for individual differences of conviction.

Both Amish and Mennonite women learn to sew at a young age. They economize by designing and sewing much of the family's clothing. Frugality is also aided by skillful mending and careful care of clothing.

The wide range of patterns of dress makes it difficult to say how a Mennonite dresses. Mennonites believe in dressing simply and modestly. Some wear distinctive attire which includes for men straight-cut coats with no lapels and no neckties.

Women wear capes over their simply designed dresses with long sleeves and skirts below the knee.

Less conservative Mennonite men wear lapel coats, neckties, and shirts in keeping with current fashions. Women wear dresses made from current patterns. Some younger members wear slacks, culottes, and informal attire for sports and certain kinds of work. However, slacks and shorts for women generally do not meet with the approval of church leaders nor with many of the parents. Patterns of dress vary widely, even among young people. Many dress modestly and decently, though not necessarily distinctively.

The Amish adhere to more uniform clothing customs. Dress becomes a visible symbol which strengthens group loyalty. One can never forget one's Amish identity while wearing the distinctive garb. Men wear suits of dark fabric, straight-cut coat with no lapels, broadfall trousers, solid-colored shirts, and black footwear. Hooks and eyes replace buttons on the suit coat and vest. An Amishman usually wears a hat when outside the house. The straw hat in summer replaces the black broadbrimmed one worn in other seasons. Men do not follow hair fads, which come and go, but continue a uniform haircut with the length about to the middle of the ear. Married men let their beards grow, but they do not grow mustaches. A moustache is considered unsanitary and they may object to its former association with the military.

Amish women design and sew most of the men's clothing, as well as their own. They purchase fabrics, stockings, shoes, hats, and underwear from local stores. They make women's dresses and men's shirts from plain-colored fabric. They select blue, green, lavender, or white for men's shirts, and blue, green, lavender, brown, gray, or black for women's dresses. Pink may be used for children's dresses and shirts.

Principles of modesty taught in Scriptures are interpreted much more strictly by Amish than by Mennonites. Amish women wear their dresses long, reaching several inches below the knee. The woman's garb includes a cape and apron, full skirt, long sleeves, and dress full to the neck. For work, sleeves may be rolled up or cut short, and an apron from the waist down with no cape may suffice. The women do not wear factory-made coats.

During cold weather a heavy shawl serves as adequate protection.

Long hair and the wearing of a head covering (veiling or cap) for Amish and many Mennonite women is based on the scriptural teaching of Paul in 1 Corinthians 11:3-16:

> Now I want you to realize that the head of every man is Christ, and the head of the woman is man, and the head of Christ is God. Every man who prays or prophesies with his head covered dishonors his head. And every woman who prays or prophesies with her head uncovered dishonors her head—it is just as though her head were shaved. If a woman does not cover her head, she should have her hair cut off, and if it is a disgrace for a woman to have her hair cut or shaved off, she should cover her head. A man ought not to cover his head, since he is the image and glory of God; but the woman is the glory of man. For man did not come from woman, but woman from man; neither was man created for woman, but woman for man. For this reason, and because of the angels, the woman ought to have a sign of authority on her head.
>
> In the Lord, however, woman is not independent of man, nor is man independent of woman. But everything comes from God. Judge for yourselves: Is it proper for a woman to pray to God with her head uncovered? Does not the very nature of things teach you that if a man has long hair, it is a disgrace to him, but that if a woman has long hair, it is her glory? For long hair is given to her as a covering. . . . We have no other practice—nor do the churches of God.

Amish women all wear their hair the same way. They part it in the middle, comb the hair straight down on each side of the face, then make a tight roll along the hairline pulling it all together at the back and rolling the remainder of the hair into a bun. This hairstyle serves to keep the hair well in place. Women do not need to stop frequently to brush, comb, and fuss with their hair. It stays neat and comfortable all day.

Amish women wear a head covering of white organdy, shaped to fit over the hair, exposing only the front part of the hair around the face. Ribbons of the same organdy material give the appearance of ties, but straight pins through the cap into the hair hold the cap firmly in place.

Amish children wear clothing which readily identifies them. Their dress and hairstyle closely imitate those of the adults.

Hairstyles for Mennonite women show more variation, as do patterns for the veiling. Some Mennonite women still wear the head covering every day, while many wear it only for public worship. Others do not wear it at all.

Amish children wear clothing which readily identifies them. Their dress closely imitates that of the adults. Even little ones not yet members by choice belong to the Amish tradition and not to "the world." It probably makes it easier for them to join the church when they do not need to change their appearance abruptly. Mennonite children generally appear much like their neighbors, although principles of modesty and simplicity influence their attire.

5

Religious Life
and
Worship

A Sunday morning drive past an Amish farm may delight the observer who sees a large number of Amish carriages in the lane and around the buildings. This scene indicates that one of the county's one hundred Amish church districts has convened for worship. About thirty-five families make up a district. They gather every two weeks in the home of a member for preaching. The Sunday forenoon service lasts about three hours.

Preparation for the occasion includes special cleaning, removal of carpets and furniture, and perhaps taking out a partition. Men and women sit separately on backless benches arranged in rows. The host family provides chairs for visitors and elderly folks. In summertime the benches and chairs may be set on a well-swept barn floor.

The worship begins with the singing of hymns from the *Ausbund,* an old German hymnbook. The book contains words but no scores of music. A leader starts a hymn, and after he sings a syllable, others join in. The unison singing, unaccompanied, resembles a chant. The second hymn is always a hymn of praise, *Das Lobsang,* "The Praise Song." Here is its first verse:

O God, our Father, Thee we praise,
    And laud Thy gracious blessings,
Which Thou, O Lord, so graciously
    Anew hast manifested;
And us together, Lord, hast led,
    Us to admonish by Thy Word;
Thy grace to this end give us.
          —Leenaerdt Clock, translated by J. C. Wenger

One minister preaches a short sermon, then reminds the people of their prayer responsibilities and opportunities. The congregation kneels for silent prayer. After prayer the deacon reads from the Scripture. If no deacon is present, a minister reads, and the main sermon follows. Leaders read Scripture in High German. But they preach and admonish in Pennsylvania Dutch, more correctly identified as Pennsylvania German, which combines Palatinate German and English.

The main sermon continues for over an hour. It spans nearly the whole Bible from Adam to Christ. Following the sermon, the other ordained men give assent and take from three to ten minutes each to add their comments. Finally the minister leads in a lengthy prayer from a prayer book. The order of service varies little from time to time.

An impressive number of young people attend the preaching service. The restlessness of small children may be alleviated by serving crackers and water. Mothers carry sleeping babies to an upstairs bedroom.

After dismissal, the host family serves lunch, and all enjoy a grand time of fellowship and visiting. The only dishes and utensils for each guest are a cup and saucer, water glass, and knife. The lunch consists of coffee, two or more kinds of cheese, homemade bread, homemade butter, honey and peanut butter mixed, and a relish. This menu is standard with slight variation. If only one kind of cheese is served, there may be schnitz pie.

Men eat first and go in by age, starting with the oldest. Not everyone can be served at one time. After all have eaten, the close neighbors of the host family assume the responsibility for washing the dishes. Families then go home, except for close relatives who stay to visit and enjoy a full-course evening meal.

Most Mennonites engage in both Sunday school and preaching every Sunday. For Sunday school the entire congregation divides into classes by age level or interest groups. The Bible is the basic text and is usually supplemented by a guidebook based on the International Sunday School Lessons, or some other topical guide.

Sunday school begins at 9:00 or 9:30 a.m. and preaching service concludes about two hours later. Traditionally men and women sat separately. In many congregations families now sit together. Mennonites preach in English. Their spirited, a cappella singing, in English, brings to life the messages the writers intended to convey in their hymns. For congregational singing most Mennonites use one or more of the following: *The Mennonite Hymnal, Church Hymnal, Life Songs No. 2, Church and Sunday School Hymnal, Sing and Rejoice!* and *Hymnal: A Worship Book.*

Mennonite and Amish churches are divided into units known as districts. An Amish district is comprised of about thirty-five families who meet in the homes of members of that unit. Geographical boundaries always determine the extent of the districts. Each district has one or more ministers and a deacon.

For Mennonites, the congregations worshiping at several (or as many as ten) locations make up a district. Mennonites choose where they will attend. Each district has at least one bishop, and each congregation one or more ministers, and in some cases a deacon.

Amish bishops, ministers, and deacons are chosen by lot from the membership. Mennonite church leaders are sometimes chosen by lot, but the trend is toward using a discernment process other than the lot. The Scripture cited as a basis for using the lot is Acts 1:15-26. In this account the apostles used the lot and chose Matthias to replace Judas.

When a congregation decides to call a minister, bishop, or

Amish hold their worship services in homes of their members and park their buggies in the barnyard.

deacon by lot, a time is announced when the members will give nominations. Those nominated submit to an examining session with the bishops. All those found willing and qualified are placed in the lot.

At the ordination service the candidates sit on the first bench. The officiating bishop assigns two persons to go to another room, where one places the ordination slip in a hymnal; the second person carries the hymnals back to the bishop. The bishop places the identical hymnals upright on a pulpit or table. No one knows which one contains the slip. In an atmosphere of prayer and suspense, each candidate steps up and takes a hymnal. The bishop proceeds to open each hymnal until he comes to the one with the paper in it.

On one side of the ordination slip the words of Proverbs 16:33

Mennonites gather in large meetinghouses and arrive for church in late-model automobiles.

(KJV) read, "The lot is cast into the lap; but the whole disposing thereof is of the Lord." The other side says, "By revelation of God _____ has been chosen minister (bishop or deacon), in the Mennonite Church on _____ (date). 1 Peter 5:1-4; Acts 20:28." The ordination of the person chosen follows immediately. If the people nominate only one person, they do not need the lot. Amish ordained leaders are always men. Mennonite leaders are usually men.

Traditionally no special education was thought necessary for the ministry. Among the Mennonites many ministers feel the need for higher education in order to communicate effectively, and they frequently obtain some formal training. Most ordained persons receive no salary, but the congregation gives them support. Congregations differ in the amount and in the manner in which they provide this remuneration.

Amish congregations observe communion twice a year as part of a Sunday service. Mennonites usually do likewise. However, recently some Mennonites observe communion on special occasions in addition to the customary spring and fall times. Ordained persons or other church leaders distribute the emblems of bread and grape juice. The Amish use fermented wine. Mennonites and Amish believe that these emblems symbolize the broken body and shed blood of Christ. Participation in this Lord's Supper provides a way for Christians to express gratitude to Christ for his sacrificial love shown on Calvary and for saving them from condemnation. While serving as a memorial, the emblems also symbolize the forward look to Christ coming again.

Communion also emphasizes the fellowship of the church as the body of Christ, suffering together, if need be. The individual is bonded to the group and gives up self-will. This concept is often illustrated by comparison with the kernels of grain which are ground into one flour and bread, and with the separate grapes which are crushed to give juice for the one cup.

Mennonites and Amish wash one another's feet before or following the communion service in accord with Christ's teaching in John 13. Jesus washed the disciples' feet and told them, "So if I, your Lord and Teacher, have washed your feet, you also ought to wash one another's feet. For I have set you an example, that you also should do as I have done to you. Very truly, I tell you, servants are not greater than their master, nor are messengers greater than the one who sent them. If you know these things, you are blessed if you do them" (John 13:14-17, NRSV). In literal practice today of Christ's directive, participants symbolize humility, love, and willingness to serve one another.

Baptism marks an important event in the life of every Amish and Mennonite youth. Baptism follows the experience of conversion. Applicants for baptism recognize their sinful state, confess past sins and repent of them, and accept the death of Jesus as a sacrifice for their sins. They remember the Scripture where "Peter replied, 'Repent and be baptized, every one of you, in the name of Jesus Christ so that your sins may be forgiven. And you will receive the gift of the Holy Spirit' " (Acts 2:38).

In baptism an ordained leader pours water on the head three times as the bishop speaks, "I baptize you with water in the name of the Father, Son, and Holy Ghost." Mennonite youth are nurtured in the faith community. In their early teens, many publicly confess Christ as Savior, are baptized, and officially join the church. Amish youth usually receive baptism after age sixteen. Applicants for baptism undergo a period of instruction in which they are taught the doctrines and discipline of the church.

Mennonites teach that one can know that one has eternal life. In times past a person who has expressed assurance of salvation might have been considered boastful. Not so today. However, the Amish tend to retain this older attitude.

If Amish members break their baptismal vow, the church excommunicates them and places them under the ban. This means that other members will not eat at the same table or transact business with them. The practice of the ban, or shunning, is based on the scriptural passage in 1 Corinthians 5:11 (NRSV): "But now I am writing to you not to associate with anyone who bears the name of brother or sister who is sexually immoral or greedy, or is an idolater, reviler, drunkard, or robber. Do not even eat with such a one." In the Mennonite Church excommunication bans one from sharing at the communion "table." In either case, the church intends the ban to encourage the backslider to repent and return to a position of fellowship among the believers.

While the Amish have no formal Sunday school, they do have a strong program of Bible teaching in the home. The parents take their responsibility seriously. The family often is studying the Word during the forenoons of religious holidays and on the Sunday when they do not have preaching. They visit friends and relatives in the afternoons of these special days.

Religious life affects activities throughout the week and governs the total lifestyle to a large extent.

6

Courtship,
Weddings,
and Funerals

Some visitors have the idea that an Amish farmer paints his gates blue to announce that he has a marriageable daughter; that is completely untrue. Marriage outside the Amish faith is forbidden, and everyone in the church knows the status of everyone else. So what need to advertise!

Courtship and Weddings

The Amish consider courtship a secretive matter. On the alternate Sunday when they have church, the youth gather for singing in the evening. A boy may bring his sister, or meet his girlfriend at some agreed-upon point. Even couples going steady mix with the crowd and court alone only after the singing when the young man takes the girl to her home in his open buggy. This buggy with no top is known as the courting buggy. (The family carriage has the gray sides and top.) The boy may visit the girl's home the week between church Sundays on a Saturday night and spend a few hours with her in the sitting room. The Amish sitting room, what most Americans would call the living room, serves especially as a guest room. It is not used as regularly as the typical living room most people know.

When a couple decides to marry, they have their names "published" at the Sunday morning service just prior to the time of weddings in the fall. Weddings are all-day celebrations held on Tuesdays or Thursdays, usually in November. The Amish print no formal invitations. Friends and relatives receive word-of-mouth invitations. From 200 to 300 guests arrive at the bride's home around 8:30 a.m. If the bride's home is too small, a nearby relative or neighbor within her church district will host the celebration.

The backless benches used for Sunday services are brought in, and men and women sit separately in straight rows. The bride and groom sit facing each other with the women in the room behind the bride and the men in the room behind the groom. Each has two witnesses.

The bride wears a dress the color of her choice—usually plain blue, lavender, or green with white organdy cape and apron. After that day she will wear a black cape and apron. The white one will be laid away and worn only for her burial. In most districts the bride wears a black prayer cap. This is the last time she wears the black covering, which she has worn only for Sunday worship since about age thirteen. She changes to the white prayer cap the afternoon of her wedding day. (In the Lower Pequea districts, they no longer wear the black prayer veil.)

The wedding service continues until around noon. Everyone joins in singing hymns from the *Ausbund*. Several ministers speak and read before the bishop preaches the main sermon. Near the end of the sermon he asks the couple to come forward. The groom walks slightly ahead of the bride, and the two stand before the bishop to take their vows. After the couple sit down, facing each other as before, the bishop concludes his sermon and allows for testimonies. Ordained men and older male relatives of the couple each speak, adding about a half hour more to

Courtship and wedding practices for Mennonites (above) correspond to those of Christians of other denominations. Great variety exists from the simple to the elaborate. Amish weddings (not pictured) follow the strict traditions of their group.

the length of the service. After the benediction the boys and men go outside, bridegroom included; the bride, girls, and women go upstairs. Then those couples who have been assigned the honor of cooking swing into action to prepare the tables for the wedding feast.

When all is ready, the young folks along with the newlyweds come into the house and take their places at the first sitting. The bride and groom sit at a corner table situated where they can best see a good number of the guests. They stay seated while the next two groups come in to eat. Cooks clear the tables, then reset them for the second and third groups. The cooks eat last.

The meal consists of fowl which has been cooked on the bone and the meat taken off and mixed with filling (made from home-made bread), then baked in the oven. The menu also includes stewed celery, mashed potatoes, vegetables, applesauce, relishes, doughnuts, pie, and cookies.

During the afternoon people sit around tables and sing. Cold food for snacks graces the tables. At supper the girls are upstairs waiting anxiously when the boys come in to select girls to accompany them to the table. Those who have regular girlfriends lead out. The boy takes a girl by the hand and leads her to the table. Other couples hesitantly match up, with some persuasion and suggestions from friends, and join the other couples at the table. Again food abounds, with the main attraction being beautifully decorated layer cakes baked by the bride's friends. After supper the guests stay to visit and sing until after eleven o'clock.

An initiation takes place the next day when the newlyweds must wash all the tablecloths and tea towels used for the wedding feasts.

Guests do not take gifts to the wedding, but give them to the couple when they visit in their homes in the weeks that follow. They give simple and practical items.

Courting and wedding practices for Mennonites correspond to those of Christians of other denominations. A great variation exists from the simple to the elaborate wedding. The ceremony customarily held in the church meetinghouse includes a short sermon and frequently singing by a quartet or other special music ensemble. A reception at a banquet hall or restaurant generally follows.

Marriage vows are taken seriously by Mennonites and Amish. Divorce is out—particularly for the Amish. Rarely does one hear of a separation among the Amish. This cannot be so definitely stated about Mennonites, although they do not look with favor upon separation and divorce.

Funerals

Amish funerals are conducted in a uniform manner, illustrating again the idea of equality and lack of status among brothers and sisters. The cost of one funeral varies little from the cost of the next. The same kind of coffin serves all, only differing in size. The pattern for the coffin was brought from Europe and continues to be made by the tradesman in Lancaster County for the benefit of the Amish. The coffin is six-sided extending out to a point about a third of the way from the top. From there the two top parts fold back so the top part of the body can be viewed. A local funeral director embalms the body. About 95 percent of the Amish patronize one particular funeral director. The family clothes the body with the same style of clothing the person wore in life, except that all of the garments are white.

The Amish always hold the funeral service three days after the death, unless this falls on Sunday or a wedding day for someone in the district. It is always held in the home—never in the funeral parlor. They place the coffin across the doorway of the room. The immediate family sits in one room behind the coffin facing it. The other relatives sit in the room opposite, facing the other side of the coffin. Another room accommodates the nonrelative church members, friends, and neighbors. The ministers sit on a bench near the coffin on the side where the relatives sit. Several ministers participate in the 90-minute service. They read a hymn but do not sing. Everyone present passes by the coffin on the side opposite the immediate family for viewing.

Lunch is served in the home. Those going to the cemetery eat first. (Occasionally Amish hold funerals in the afternoon and serve no lunch. When this is the case, family and friends eat together after the burial.) The funeral director leads the procession in his station wagon. Next follows the horse-drawn hearse driven by an Amishman. The procession proceeds at about five to six miles per hour. Everyone views the body again at the cemetery, with the family viewing it last. Four pallbearers lower the coffin and cover it with earth while the family watches.

The Amish display little outward emotion throughout the service. They place no flowers on the grave. The tombstones, simple in structure, not large, and much alike, again point out the lack of one having higher status than another. Both the Amish and Mennonites believe in the resurrection which the Bible promises to believers. Only the body, not the soul, rests in the cemetery.

Mennonites generally ask that flowers be omitted, but otherwise funerals differ little from those of other Christian churches in Lancaster County. They usually hold an hour-long service in the church, followed by a short committal with no viewing at the grave. Those officiating read from the Scripture at each service. Frequently the congregation or a small group sing in the church and sometimes at the graveside. Mennonites usually hold a viewing at the funeral parlor the evening before the funeral. They also view in the church either before or after the formal service. In some cases families prefer to hold the service in the funeral home.

7

Education

The traditional "Little Red Schoolhouse" of the early 1900s has been preserved by the Amish as the place to teach their young ones the three R's. The churches operate approximately ninety parochial schools, taught almost exclusively by Amish teachers. All members share in the operating expense of the schools in accordance with their ability to pay. The burden does not fall so heavily, then, on families of school-age children. In addition, the Amish pay property taxes to support public schools just as do their non-Amish neighbors. An Amish school board chooses teachers on the basis of their ability to learn and aptitude for teaching. Usually young women with only eighth-grade education accept this responsibility, although occasionally a man teaches. The teachers get together once a month to discuss problems and exchange ideas on teaching.

The Amish send attendance records to the state. Otherwise

The Amish operate about ninety one-room schools in Lancaster County. Amish children do not go to high school.

the state rarely checks on the schools or interferes in any way. Subjects in the early grades include reading, writing, arithmetic, and spelling. Teachers also encourage artwork, singing, and play. German reading begins in third grade.

Consolidation of schools sparked the era of parochial schools. The Amish felt that the consolidated school would interfere with their remaining a separate people. Mennonites also opposed the consolidation in the beginning.

Amish children do not go into high school. To meet the requirements of compulsory education to age fifteen, the youth who finish eighth grade receive agricultural and domestic training at home and attend a three-hour session of vocational school on Saturday. Youth from the area meet in a one-room school to receive instruction in arithmetic, spelling, German and English reading, and German singing. A teacher who is responsible for all eight grades in one of the schools during the week often assumes the additional responsibility of the vocational school. It was the writer's privilege recently to visit one of the Saturday schools. The math book used was titled *Arithmetic in Agriculture*. The children sang German in unison, with the teacher voicing the first note before the children joined in, singing slowly just as they do in church.

The education received by Amish children in school is strongly supported with practical training and work experience at home. These together quite adequately prepare them for life as they know it. To them, public high school seems irrelevant and would not help them to remain a separate people.

For Mennonites, education takes a slightly different turn. Many attend the public schools, while an increasing number attend Mennonite schools. The Mennonites have fourteen or more elementary schools in or near Lancaster County, with well over 2,500 pupils. Lancaster Mennonite High School started in 1942 and now has around 700 students. These schools are attended by children from the Atlantic Coast Mennonite Conference and the Beachy Amish, along with children from the Lancaster Mennonite Conference. A small but increasing number of children from non-Mennonite families also attend.

Recently a conservative element of Mennonites operate Faith

Mennonites sponsor fourteen or more elementary schools in the Lancaster area. Lancaster Mennonite High School has over 700 students. Mennonites frequently go on to college and graduate school.

Mennonite High School near Gap, Pennsylvania, with 100 or less students. Even later, a similar group of Mennonites opened the Terre Hill Mennonite High School with around 100 students. The Mennonite and Amish schools receive some support from the church but depend largely on tuition. Members patronizing their own schools continue to pay taxes for public schools.

Mennonites see higher education as increasingly important and acceptable. The opportunities involved in entering the service professions present a challenge. Lancaster County has no

Mennonite colleges. However, Eastern Mennonite College at Harrisonburg, Virginia, enrolls a large number from the Lancaster area and also has an extension program at Lancaster. Some students go to Goshen College, a Mennonite college in Indiana. A considerable number of youth also attend the local Millersville State College, as well as colleges in other places. Eastern Mennonite Seminary, also at Harrisonburg, attracts students from Lancaster County, including women.

Mennonites and Amish do not limit their education to the formal schoolroom. Parents feel the responsibility for teaching their children in domestic, agricultural, and trade skills as well as in religion. In addition to home and school, the Mennonite Church assists in religious education through Sunday schools, Bible schools, adult education classes, seminars, camps, retreats, and other special meetings.

Not all Mennonites in Lancaster County look with enthusiasm on higher education. Some who do not support higher education feel it causes young people to leave the farm—which many firmly believe is still the ideal place to rear a family.

The range in education among Mennonites includes those who feel no need to go beyond eighth grade to those who continue postgraduate studies after earning one or more degrees. A considerable number of Amish and Mennonites are self-educated. Without formal higher education, they continue to read and become knowledgeable in many fields.

8

Economics
and
Occupations

"If I lived here, I could live close to God, too. Life is so peaceful and unhurried." Frequently a city visitor to the country expresses this attitude.

God dwells in the hearts of people rather than in a particular place. But rural life does have its advantages. Amish and Mennonites thrive well on it. Hard work and thrift together with a heritage of skill in agriculture combine to make successful farmers. In Europe, the Amish were entirely an agricultural people. Their value system calls for a farmer to manage well and save in order to buy farms for his children.

Amish attach great importance to working the soil and remaining close to nature. They strongly prefer farming over any other occupation, but engage in other jobs and trades when necessary. They work for carpenters, painters, mason contractors, lumber companies, and other related industries in the area.

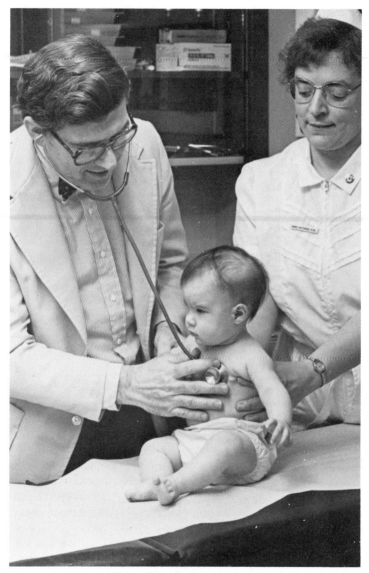

Mennonites were traditionally a rural people, but now they are employed in most of the industries, business establishments, and professions in Lancaster County.

Some are self-employed as builders, contractors, blacksmiths, harness shopkeepers, furniture craftsmen, printers, clock-makers, carriage makers, and shoe repairmen.

Nonfarm jobs and other cottage industries such as quiltmaking and handicrafts cause some concern among the Amish. These businesses take them away from farming, put them more in touch with the outside world, and encourage competition. On the other hand, they do provide needed income and help to keep families together when farming is difficult.

Mennonites make up an increasingly smaller part of the rural population in Lancaster County. However, the existing modern and progressive farms operated by Mennonites remain a significant factor in the county's agricultural picture. The range of employment for Mennonites includes most of the professions, industries, and business establishments in Lancaster County.

Labor unions create a problem for a nonresistant Christian. The "I'll get what I want even if I have to go on strike to get it" philosophy conflicts with the teaching in Scripture to "be content with your pay" (Luke 3:14). Striking also appears to violate the principle of nonviolence. An Amish or Mennonite person may refuse certain jobs if union membership is compulsory.

The Amish continue many of the older methods of farming carried over from Europe. They attempt to remain separate from the world in this as well as all other areas of life. Gasoline and diesel engines rather than electricity supply power for milking machines and milk coolers. Horses and mules do the field work instead of tractors. For silo-filling, combining, and corn-picking operations, Amish use gasoline or diesel-powered equipment. They employ tractors with steel wheels (rubber tires are not allowed) only in and around the buildings for beltwork and power takeoff jobs. They do not use tractors for field work. Horses pull any powered equipment in the field. A gasoline engine mounted on a chassis pulled by horses furnishes power for any operation in the field which requires power takeoff.

Diesel power furnishes air pressure for small equipment such as drills, saws, and fans. One Amish farmer mounted a large airplane propeller on a tractor run by gasoline. The fan served as an air conditioner to cool several thousand chickens housed in modern layer cages during warm humid weather.

The Amish can carry on their type of farming only as long as they can buy horse-drawn equipment. Since the larger manufacturers no longer produce such farm implements, it is not certain what the Amish will do about this problem in the future.

In the part of the county where the Amish live, the average size of a farm is about 60 acres. Farms there range in size from 25 to 100 acres. In parts west and south, away from Amish country, the farms are larger, about 75 to 125 acres.

Farmers find it economical to specialize. They may choose dairy, poultry, beef cattle, potato, or tomato farming. Vegetable growing in a specialized way serves nearby city markets. In another kind of operation, farmers serve as dealers in hay, straw, and corn, or in livestock.

Main crops in the county in order of acreage are corn, hay, wheat, tobacco, soybeans, barley, potatoes, and other vegetables. Farmers also grow various grasses for grazing. Corn, grain, and hay crops usually stay on the farm for feeding livestock. Tobacco, potatoes, some grain and hay, and vegetables are raised for marketing.

People sometimes wonder why the Amish and Mennonites raise tobacco. In recent years knowledge about the hazards of smoking has caused many farmers to consider this aspect of their work. Some conclude that they can raise other crops and suffer no financial loss. However, many Amish and some Mennonites continue to raise tobacco. Their fathers raised it. It is a good cash crop. It provides lucrative employment for the family during winter months when they have time for stripping tobacco. On the whole, they do not condone smoking.

Many people wonder about the wealth of Amish farmers because they do not spend money for many of the modern conveniences and luxuries of the society around them. Actually, they are not particularly wealthy if wealth is counted by money in the bank. If an Amish farmer has any excess money after meeting the family's needs, he saves it to invest in more land.

The Amish recognize the quality of the land and know its value. One of the main reasons for soaring prices of land in eastern Lancaster County lies in the fact that acreage next to farms Am-

Although Amish refuse to use modern equipment, their farms are among the finest in Pennsylvania.

ish already own is more valuable than land at some distant point. They want their children to be farmers. They have no cars. The families can communicate with one another better (without telephones) if not scattered too widely. And they do not have so far to travel to church if the homes of members are close together.

A farmer will pay a high price for a farm, but will usually sell it to his son for less. By hard work the son will build credit and can borrow money elsewhere to pay back his dad at least in part. Then the father can buy another farm. An unwritten rule holds that if an Amishman has one farm half paid and owns the implements and livestock, his credit allows him to buy another farm. Other reasons for the high prices of land are the housing developments, highways, schools, and industries necessary to accommodate an increasing population.

Amish and Mennonites pay income taxes, and most Mennonites pay Social Security tax. Amish secure an exemption from paying Social Security if they are self-employed or work for fellow Amish. The exception for them comes about as a result of their belief about taking care of their own people. Elderly parents become the charges of the children. Parents work hard to rear their children, save to buy homes or farms for them, and teach them to live frugally. In turn, the children respect their parents and consider it their God-given responsibility to take care of them. Rarely will an Amish person take residence in an old people's home. Seldom do they accept Social Security benefits or Medicare.

However, the rural community no longer supports all of them on the land. Some find gainful employment in local industry and by virtue of this have become a part of the Social Security program and benefits.

One only needs to view the landscape to see that farmers take great pride in neat, well-kept farms. Even fencerows, trees, and pastureland receive the farmer's skillful care. Contour farming prevents excess erosion. Crop rotation helps conserve the soil from being depleted of certain minerals. Farmers carefully study how to use and not abuse the valuable land.

Both Amish and Mennonite farmers take advantage of scientific finds regarding weed and insect control. They use commercially prepared fertilizers. They spray and apply the various preparations for control of insects and other pests. They appreciate and benefit from the help provided by Pennsylvania State University through its Agriculture Extension Service.

9

The Way of Love
and
Sharing

A New Jersey visitor commented that the men in quaint attire with long flowing beards looked like the elves in the story about the shoemaker. With hammer and nails they worked swiftly and skillfully, thick as flies on the huge skeleton barn.

He was referring to barn raising, which usually follows a barn fire. Or a new additional barn may be going up. Amish and Mennonites believe in helping each other. Special loyalty is shown within the membership, but their love and sharing also extend to neighbors near and far.

Amish do not take insurance from commercial companies, with the exception of farm liability. They carry this in case their animals cause an accident. Their concern for one another does not allow the one who suffers financial misfortune to bear the burden alone. They take care of fire and storm damage expenses through the Amish Aid Society. Money is paid into this treasury

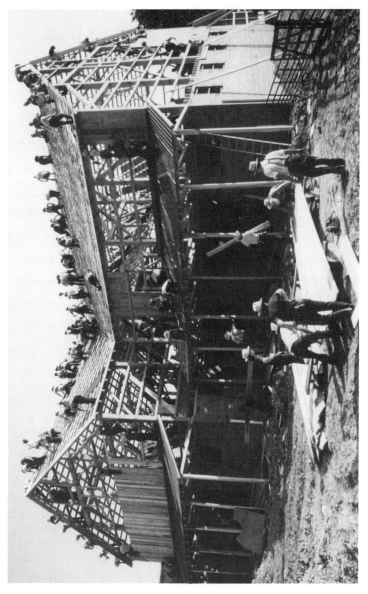

Amish do not carry commercial insurance. A barn raising is an example of how they share with each other in times of special need.

in accordance with losses and the ability of members to contribute. This organization extends to Amish communities beyond Lancaster County. Some districts keep a hospitalization fund working among themselves.

Mennonites generally carry automobile, fire, and hospitalization insurance. Mennonite Mutual Aid serves a large number for hospitalization. Mennonites also operate Mennonite Mutual Fire Insurance Association and a Brotherly Aid Liability insurance for automobiles. However, many members choose to carry various kinds of insurance offered by larger commercial companies. Many also accept insurance as a fringe benefit at their places of employment.

Hurricane Agnes in 1972 brought into public light the work of Mennonite Disaster Service (MDS). Vans and cars carried hundreds of Amish and Mennonite volunteers to help shovel mud, mop, scrub, clean, and later rebuild homes of flood victims in surrounding areas. Congregational contact men cooperate with the national MDS director at Akron, Pennsylvania, in recruiting volunteers. Storms, floods, earthquakes, and fires which trigger disaster for fellow humans call MDS into action.

Closely related to MDS is Mennonite Central Committee (MCC), which also has its home base at Akron, Pennsylvania. MCC is the relief and service agency of North America Mennonite and Brethren in Christ churches. Founded in 1920, it administers and participates in programs of agricultural and economic development, education, medicine, self-help, relief, and peace in fifty countries.

MCC grew out of the desire of Mennonite churches to respond to urgent human need and to testify by service to the gospel of love and peace. Its programs seek to reflect the compassion of Jesus to teach the good news to the poor, to proclaim release for the captives and recovery of sight for the blind, and to set at liberty those who are oppressed. MCC has more than 1,000 persons (including many from Lancaster County) serving in Africa, Asia, Europe, North America, and South America. MCC personnel try to erase barriers that separate people from each other and from God. MCC is dedicated to reconciliation in the name of Christ.

Mennonites and Amish believe in a nonresistant way of life. Jesus said, "Love your enemies, bless them that curse you, do good to them that hate you, and pray for them which despitefully use you, and persecute you" (Matthew 5:44, KJV). God gave life. Only God may take life.

Mennonites and Amish object to all wars. This position has brought severe persecution at times in the past. However, in recent wars Mennonites and others who took a conscientious objector stand for reasons of religious conviction were granted special concessions. An alternate service program provided a way for young men to serve in constructive programs in this country and overseas. Amish usually obtained farm deferments.

Mennonites and Amish believe in nonresistance rather than simply in pacifism. A pacifist may oppose war merely on a moral or humanistic basis. Nonresistant conscientious objectors oppose war because of biblical principles which they cannot violate. This conviction for nonviolence and peacemaking reaches into all areas of life and marks those who are like God in character: "Blessed are the peacemakers, for they will be called the children of God" (Matthew 5:9, NRSV).

On the basis of 1 Corinthians 6:1, lawsuits are forbidden: "If any of you has a dispute with another, dare he take it before the ungodly for judgment instead of before the saints?" Verse seven in the same chapter says, "The very fact that you have lawsuits among you means you have been completely defeated already. Why not rather be wronged? Why not rather be cheated?"

Christ's Sermon on the Mount also reflects the spirit of nonviolence. In Matthew 5:39-41 Jesus instructs his followers, "But I say to you, Do not resist an evildoer. But if anyone strikes you on the right cheek, turn the other also; and if anyone wants to sue you and take your coat, give your cloak as well; and if anyone forces you to go one mile, go also the second mile" (NRSV).

Occasionally someone asks what a nonresistant person would do in a crisis where self-defense seems necessary. Each Christian needs to answer this for oneself. Some measure of self-defense may be legitimate—especially preventive measures. However, to kill another to defend one's country, family, or self would be to contradict the clear teaching of Christ. Furthermore, those

Mennonite and Amish volunteers respond to natural disasters, helping stricken communities clean up and rebuild damaged homes.

who have their sins forgiven and live by faith do not fear death. They believe God will take care of them and that "in all things God works for the good of those who love him, who have been called according to his purpose" (Romans 8:28).

The apostle Paul writes, " 'Vengeance is mine, I will repay, says the Lord.' No, 'if your enemies are hungry, feed them; if they are thirsty, give them something to drink; for by doing this you will heap burning coals on their heads' " (Romans 12:19-20, NRSV).

A large portion of tax money goes for military costs, and this poses a dilemma for nonresistant Christians. Amish and Mennonites generally pay taxes. The Bible again furnishes direction. Romans 13 speaks of the Christian's duty to respect and be subject to government powers. Verses six and seven say, "For the same reason you also pay taxes, for the authorities are God's servants, busy with this very thing. Pay to all what is due them—taxes to whom taxes are due, revenue to whom revenue is due, respect to whom respect is due, honor to whom honor is due" (NRSV).

The Pharisees tried to trap Jesus when they asked him, "Is it right to pay taxes to Caesar or not?" Jesus asked to see the tribute money, noted Caesar's image and superscription, and answered, "Give to Caesar what is Caesar's, and to God what is God's" (Matthew 22:17-22). Certainly Jesus knew of wars and injustice involved in the Roman government. Most twentieth-century Mennonites take this to mean that Christians pay taxes but are not responsible for how the government uses the money.

Regarding participation in government, Mennonites and Amish feel the responsibility to pray for officials, but generally they do not hold government offices. No set policy governs the matter of voting in local, state, or national elections. Some preachers encourage voting; others strongly oppose it. Members who feel strongly about an issue or candidate will likely vote if their conscience allows such action.

10

European Background

Anabaptist Beginnings

A brief look at history is essential to bring into focus the current picture of Amish and Mennonites in Lancaster County, Pennsylvania.

Mennonites and Amish trace their beginnings to January 21, 1525, in Zurich, Switzerland. The Protestant Reformation up to that point had gained much momentum under the influential leadership of Martin Luther, Ulrich Zwingli, and others. Luther and Zwingli held a new appreciation for the gospel and New Testament teachings which differed from existing state churchism. But these Reformers did not go far enough to satisfy the young men who began what developed into the Anabaptist movement.

Conrad Grebel, Georg Blaurock, and Felix Manz led out in establishing a peoplehood of believers as brothers and sisters.

They opposed baptizing infants, a practice that Zwingli had earlier called unscriptural. But to get along with the city council, Zwingli did not challenge infant baptism. There was increased pressure from the state church for Grebel and his companions to conform, and they felt it necessary to make a complete break. At a meeting in Zurich, these zealous young men baptized each other, finalizing their break from the state church.

The name Anabaptist, meaning *rebaptizers,* was given to the brothers and sisters by their enemies. They believed that one should be baptized only upon confession of faith as a responsible adult, and that the atoning work of Christ covered innocent children. They not only believed infant baptism unnecessary, but dangerous because it might give young people false hope.

In those early days, the group simply called themselves brethren or Swiss Brethren. The name Mennonite came later, due to the leading influence of Menno Simons of Holland, who left the Catholic priesthood to join the Anabaptist movement in 1536.

Major Tenets of Separation

Five major tenets separated the Swiss Brethren from both Roman and Reformed state churches and led them to set up a peoplehood of voluntary believers. In contrast, the state church baptized all people born in a certain geographical location into the church which had jurisdiction there.

Bible Authority

The new group accepted the Bible as the final authority in its revelation of God and his will for man. The New Testament established the directives for Christian ethics, policies, and practices for the church.

Adult or Believers Baptism

These brothers and sisters believed (as do their direct descendants, the Amish and Mennonites) that new Testament baptism follows an expression of faith, repentance, confession, and commitment. An innocent child cannot meet these requirements.

Separation of Church and State

The Swiss Brethren believed that the civil authorities had no right to control the church. Neither did they feel that the church should ask the state to take any part in punishing dissenters and heretics. The nonconforming believers were subjected to much persecution. Many were martyred as a result of their firm stand on this matter. Consequently there arose a strong negative attitude toward a state church structure. Anabaptists felt that a Christian could not take part in civil government. They taught that it was wrong for a follower of Christ to take any government position that involved violence in any form.

Community of Saints

This new group believed strongly that the church is the body of Christ made up only of persons who have become dedicated disciples of Christ by faith through conversion, repentance, and baptism. By the grace of God they intended to have a fellowship of people made holy and kept holy. The concept of Christian community prevailed, excluding any idea of rank, class, or station. They strove to make all members one unified body of sisters and brothers in Christ.

Nonresistance, the Way of Love and Peace

Neither *pacifism* nor *nonresistance* quite describes the way of love to which the early Anabaptists adhered. The Scripture says, "By this everyone will know that you are my disciple, if you have love for one another" (John 13:35, NRSV). These believers were taught to love their enemies, to do good to those who hated them, and to pray for those who despitefully used or persecuted them. This way of love was not simply a negative thing—not taking part in military endeavors—but a positive call to do good to all persons. Peace and love became a way of life.

Spread of Anabaptism and Persecution

At first Roman Catholic governing bodies executed these believers as Protestants. Authorities did not distinguish between Anabaptist and Protestant heresy. Later the Anabaptists suffered at the hands of Protestant governments. The first death by Protestants was the drowning of Felix Manz in Switzerland on January 5, 1527. Grounds for such extreme persecution were either the refusal to obey a government injunction not to baptize or simply turning to Anabaptism, thus transforming a religious offense into a civil one.

A significant meeting of Anabaptist leaders followed in February 1527 in Schleitheim. The threatened disintegration of the movement appears to have been prevented as they united around seven articles of agreement later referred to as the Schleitheim Confession of Faith. Michael Sattler played a leading role in the drafting of this agreement. Shortly thereafter Sattler and thirteen other Anabaptists were arrested, questioned, and tortured. Sattler was charged with intent to overthrow the Roman Catholic Church and the civil order. Officials set a heavy guard around the prison because of his popularity. Sattler met death by being burned at the stake after severe torture. His wife was executed by drowning. Approximately five thousand Anabaptists died as martyrs during those early years.

In spite of severe persecution, great missionary zeal characterized the Anabaptist movement. It spread rapidly from Switzerland into Germany and Holland. A number of new leaders arose at various places somewhat independent of one another. Consequently the movement was not completely united throughout. European Anabaptist leaders included Pilgram Marpeck, Hans Denk, Hans Hut, Jakob Hutter, Melchior Hofmann, Obbe and Dirk Philips, and the noted Dutch leader Menno Simons.

Menno Simons

Born in Witmarsum in Friesland of parents who likely were farmers, Menno Simons studied for the priesthood and was ordained in 1524. But some practices of the Roman Catholic Church troubled him. Upon careful study of the Bible, Menno concluded that infant baptism was not scriptural. He found another fallacy in the belief that the flesh and blood of Christ were physically present in the bread and wine of the mass.

Menno Simons remained in the priesthood for a while and became well known as an evangelical preacher in his hometown of Witmarsum. After much inner struggle, he publicized his new commitment to Christ on January 30, 1536, more than ten years after the Anabaptist beginnings in Zurich. Menno found fellowship with the Anabaptists. They helped him during a time of hiding when he spent much time delving into the Scriptures. He worked out his position carefully and stood firmly on it thereafter. After serious consideration he consented to become a leader and elder of the Anabaptists upon their request in 1537.

The leadership of Menno Simons, during a difficult time of persecution from without as well as struggles resulting from extremes within, saved the Dutch Anabaptist movement from succumbing to the many pressures upon it. The followers of Menno were called *Mennists* by 1545, and the name *Mennonite* continues a result of the influence and prolific writings of Menno Simons.

The Amish Division

A major concern of the early Mennonites was to keep a pure church. Those who sinned fell under severe censure. The church excommunicated them if they did not repent after being admonished twice in secret, in accordance with Matthew 18. Those so dealt with were placed under the *ban*. Considerable discussion arose concerning this practice, and there was serious disagreement. Some thought the banned persons should be shunned in all social and economic relations while others felt the shunning should apply only to the spiritual fellowship and eating at the communion table.

Starting in Switzerland, Jakob Ammann succeeded in gaining a following for his harsh interpretation of the ban and began a separate body during the years of 1693-97. Ammann wanted the strict enforcement of the ban while Hans Reist, a Mennonite elder (bishop), did not agree with this interpretation. As a result of difference on this and several other minor issues, the followers of Ammann worshiped separately from the rest of the Mennonites and thereafter became known as Amish.

Emigration to America

Mennonites and Amish, weary of being refugees and tenants, welcomed William Penn's invitation to come to Pennsylvania. They had endured persecution and poverty and longed for a place to live in peace with their families.

From 1710 to the end of the century, hundreds of Amish and Mennonites settled in southeastern Pennsylvania along the streams in fertile valleys. Areas selected in Lancaster County resembled the Rhine Palatinate from which many had come. (An immigration of Dutch Mennonites arrived at Germantown, Pennsylvania, as early as 1683.) Other German immigrants who help complete the picture of what we now refer to as the Pennsylvania Dutch include the Lutherans, Reformed, Moravians, Schwenkfelders, Dunkers, and Seventh-Day Baptists. All spoke German and adhered to similar culture and methods of farming.

Mennonite settlements continued to grow in Lancaster County following 1710. Later they spread west of Lancaster and into York, Adams, and Lebanon counties.

The Amish first came to America during the late 1720s and settled in Berks County, Pennsylvania. They came into Lancaster County around the early 1760s and settled east and north of the first Mennonite settlements. Today Amish can be found in almost any section east, southeast, and northeast of Lancaster city to the borders of the county.

In Europe today no Amish remain who retain the name and principles of the original group. Those who did not come to America merged with the Mennonites. At least, they lost their Amish identity.

Lancaster County hosts the oldest and best-known Amish settlement today, but not the largest. Beginning about 1800, migrations continued further west. Ohio now has the largest Amish settlement. Large numbers of Amish also live in Indiana. Amish can be found in at least nineteen other states as well as in Ontario, Canada. A number of new settlements have begun recently in several Central and South American countries.

11

Varieties of Mennonites, Amish, and Similar Groups

Gray buggies—black buggies; full beards—well-trimmed beards; black cars—painted bumpers; Amish in cars—Amish in buggies; electricity—no electricity. These and other differences contribute to the confusion about who's who among the plain folk. As stated in chapter one, the bulk of this book deals with the two largest bodies, the Lancaster Conference of the Mennonite Church and the Old Order Amish. This chapter introduces branches and historically related groups represented in Lancaster County. It also attempts to correct ideas about religious organizations in no way identified with Amish and Mennonites, but mistakenly thought to be.

Amish Groups

The Beachy Amish, named for Moses M. Beachy of Salisbury, Pennsylvania, began about 1927. Lancaster County has four congregations of these active people who also answer to the names Amish Mennonite, Church Amish, and Weavertown. The latter is the name of the original Beachy church here. They worship in meetinghouses and do not practice shunning of people who leave to join other plain or less-plain churches.

Differing from Old Orders, the Beachy Amish also allow electricity, telephones, tractors, and automobiles. Their worship services include Sunday school, English preaching, and evening meetings. They retain a plain garb similar to that of the Amish. Men trim their beards more closely.

Like Mennonites, the Beachy Amish sing a cappella in four-part harmony, using hymns and gospel songs. The Amish Mennonites, as they prefer to be called, also engage in mission outreach. A recent spiritual awakening among them set the stage for enthusiasm in witnessing. They operate their own information center as a way of sharing their faith with tourists.

A few smaller groups, sometimes referred to in a general way as New Amish, represent various departure from the Old Order. These keep the plain garb but may allow cars, electricity, meetinghouses for preaching, or other specified changes, and are generally more evangelistic. New Order Amish permit tractors in the fields but do not have cars.

Mennonite Groups

The Atlantic Coast Conference of the Mennonite Church lists nine churches in Lancaster County. In times past these churches embraced more liberal practices than Lancaster Conference. However, at present their differences appear minor and members fellowship together, visit, and take part in each others' services.

The General Conference Mennonites with headquarters in Newton, Kansas, also have a few congregations in Lancaster County. They believe much the same as the Mennonite Church, but put less emphasis on separation from others in attire.

Swinging over to the conservative side, several conferences of Mennonites began as a result of a desire to maintain a more strict interpretation of church discipline. Eastern Pennsylvania Mennonite Church has nine congregations in Lancaster County. They place more emphasis on attire and less emphasis on higher education, and are in general more conservative than Lancaster Conference Mennonites. They operate their own Christian day schools with a school for almost every congregation. They are active in missions, which are administered by their own group.

A number of earlier schisms from Lancaster Conference come under the general heading of Old Order Mennonites. Two groups emerged—the Horning Mennonites, officially Weaverland Conference Mennonites, and the Wenger Mennonites, officially Groffdale Conference Mennonites. The names *Wisler* and *Martinites* are also at times applied to both these groups. Both wear distinctive garb somewhat like the Amish, but men do not grow beards and women wear dresses with capes of matching material, either solid color or fine print. The Horning people drive black cars with even the chrome parts painted black— hence the nickname, *Black Bumpers.* However, they no longer all paint their bumpers black. The Wenger people continue to use horse and buggy. They drive black carriages—different in construction from the gray Amish buggies.

A number of smaller groups resemble the Old Order Mennonites but are separate bodies. These include the Reidenbach Mennonites and the Pikers, so named because their church stood along a certain pike (or road) and was called the Pike Church.

The Reformed Mennonites, also locally referred to as New Mennonites, began in 1812 at Strasburg, Pennsylvania, under the leadership of John Herr. He aimed to carry out the teachings of the New Testament and felt that no existing church measured up to his ideals. His father was a Mennonite, but John had not joined the church prior to his establishing the Reformed Mennonite Church. Reformed Mennonites wear an austere garb. Women wear much gray clothing, including a distinctive type of gray bonnet. They do not attend services of other denominations and have no Sunday schools or evening services. Membership is on the decline. Only one congregation remains in Lancaster County, the Longenecker Church near Strasburg.

Mennonite-Related Groups

Brethren in Christ trace their beginning to Mennonite ancestry. They became known as *River Brethren* because they practice immersion as their mode of baptism. Later they adopted the name Brethren in Christ. Like Mennonites they take the peace position and are a missionary church. They cooperate in the work of the Mennonite Central Committee. Theologically, they identify with both the Wesleyan holiness and Anabaptist positions.

The United Zion churches spring from the Brethren in Christ. A conservative branch of Brethren in Christ retains the name Old Order River Brethren. These groups enjoy a good relationship with each other. They like to say, "We can't all be Mennonites, but we can all be Brethren in Christ."

Hutterites belong to the Anabaptist family. None live in Lancaster County, but their unique practice of community of goods brings them into public interest. Lancaster bookstores sell books about the Hutterites. Approximately 361 colonies prosper in the United States and Canada, as well as one each in England, Germany, and Japan. The total membership is approximately 35,000.

Nonrelated Groups

A group of Pietists in Germany started the Church of the Brethren. They teach a simple life and nonresistance. They differ from Mennonites and Amish in baptizing by immersion and in keeping the love feast. Some of the Church of the Brethren think of themselves as coming out of the same Anabaptist stream that produced the Mennonites, although there are few direct connections.

The name Dunkard, earlier applied to the Church of the Brethren, comes from Dunker, the English rendering of *Tunker,* a German word meaning *dipper* or *immerser.* This refers to their mode of baptism. The name of the group was German Baptist until the year 1908. Two small conservative bodies retain a Dunkard name: Old Order Dunkards and Dunkard Brethren.

Again, these have few direct historical relationships with Mennonites or Amish.

Onlookers frequently confuse Amish with Quakers, who in the past wore a plain garb. The Society of Friends, their more acceptable name, trace their history to England. They began as a part of a pietistic movement under the leadership of George Fox. Similar to the early Anabaptists, the Friends lived a simple life and held the peace position. However, historians find few direct connections between the Quakers and the Anabaptists.

The Baptists trace their history to the European Anabaptists through contact with Mennonites in Amsterdam. The Baptist Church, however, was founded in England. The two groups agreed on believers baptism, but not on the matter of rejecting war and swearing oaths. The Baptists in England kept up a lively correspondence with the Dutch Mennonites for a while, but eventually there was a parting of denominational ways.

The Moravian Brethren (formerly Bohemian Brethren) organized in 1467, before the Anabaptist beginnings. Historical connections cannot be proved and are not likely. In the early days, however, the Moravians held to many of the same principles as did the Anabaptists.

The Ephrata Cloister highlights the history of another Pennsylvania German people, the Seventh-Day German Baptists. The founder, Conrad Beissel, from Germany, embraced the Dunker faith before organizing the monastic institution which no longer exists except by the historical and cultural monument preserved in the museum at Ephrata. This group has no historical or denominational connection with the Mennonites or the Amish. However, a number of Mennonites were swept into this movement, and some aspects of the German culture suggest kinship.

Mormons, also known as the Church of Jesus Christ of Latter-Day Saints, give their book of Mormon equal status with the Holy Bible. Their beliefs differ widely from those of the Anabaptist descendants. Mention of Mormons is included here solely because tourists sometimes wonder if the Mennonites are connected with them.

Another group often confused with Amish are the Amana people in Iowa. One can see some similarities between the older

Amana colonies and the German culture preserved by the Amish. However, their origin and religious beliefs bear little in common with Amish. Amana people are in no way affiliated with the Amish.

12

Evangelism
and
Missions

The simple rural lifestyle of the "plain people" attracts occasional visitors to the extent that they inquire about becoming members. Can an "outsider" join? Yes, they welcome any person who sincerely accepts the Christian faith and is willing to live within the disciplines of any particular segment of the plain people.

Few newcomers take up membership in the Amish church for obvious reasons. The "outsider," while accepted warmly as a friend, finds some barriers to feeling at home among the Amish. The culture stands in sharp contrast to society in general. It would be difficult, but not impossible, for anyone not brought up within it to survive in the culture. A few cases can be cited where an outsider married an Amish and did become an accepted part of the Amish community.

On the other hand, Mennonites and Amish have no monopoly on the "peaceful life." Most of the Mennonite fellowships want to share the good life by inviting anyone who will to accept the gospel of Jesus Christ, which is the basis for a life of peace.

The Anabaptists of the sixteenth century believed that the gospel should be preached. Only in this way would people believe, and only when they believed should they be baptized. As noted earlier, this attitude rejected the state-church idea that every person living in a certain geographical location belonged to the church which had jurisdiction there. Laypeople went out witnessing in those early days. As early as 1527 we have record of an Anabaptist Martyrs Synod in Germany which turned out to be a missionary strategy session. From there, evangelists went out to teach and extend the body of believers.

In the years that followed, missionary zeal decreased. The church succumbed to pressures of persecution and discrimination. Gradually Mennonites became known more for their traditional practices and their quiet, peaceful way of life and less for their active evangelism. This trend continued until it seemed wrong to send members out of the close community to evangelize. Along with other new things, such action Mennonites classified as worldly.

Old Order Amish along with some Old Order Mennonites have retained this position and desire to remain "the quiet in the land." However, missionary zeal experienced a strong rebirth around the beginning of this century in Mennonite circles, and more recently among the Church Amish.

The Eastern Mennonite Board of Missions and Charities at Salunga, Pennsylvania, coordinates the mission outreach for the Lancaster Conference of the Mennonite Church. It had its beginning in an organization called the Home and Mennonite Sunday School Mission Advocates, formed as a result of Bible meetings in 1894. Lancaster County Sunday School Mission replaced the Advocates, and in 1914 the Eastern Board was organized.

Eastern Mennonite Board of Missions and Charities presently serves the Lancaster Conference churches with its three departments—Overseas Ministries, Home Ministries, and Discipleship Ministries.

The Overseas Ministries department sponsors about 160 adult

Mennonite missionaries teach agricultural methods (top) as well as Bible lessons (bottom).

missionaries (and their more than 100 children) in 26 countries. These missionaries work with churches having a total membership of 60,000. The board relates to an additional nine countries with finances and administrative visits. The present relationship of the church here with overseas congregations is largely one of partnership—a brother-sister rather than a parent-child relationship. In this supportive role the board responds to requests from overseas churches and provides leadership training, medical personnel, teachers, nutrition educationists, and agricultural workers.

The experiences of the Mennonite Church in mission have caused it to take a new look at the role of culture in Christianity. The gospel must be expressed in cultural forms, but the gospel in itself transcends all cultures. Persons are saved by grace, through faith in Jesus Christ, not by participating in a "God-fearing" culture. So one finds a great diversity among Mennonites the world over in lifestyle, practices in worship, expression in art and music, and customs that constitute cultural identity. Yet faithful Christians in these diverse fellowships all experience the living presence of Jesus Christ.

On the home front, Eastern Board's Home Ministries department has approximately 110 workers serving as church planters or pastors in 11 states and the District of Columbia. Many of these serve in congregations originally started by the board. Home Ministries is also involved in creating new models for effective urban evangelism, church growth, leadership development, Jewish outreach, Mennonite Information Center, Choice Books distribution, youth and summer camp programs, and a children's visitation program. Eastern Board sees its role at home as a partner—working with congregations and districts to extend God's kingdom.

Closely related to both Overseas and Home Ministries is the Discipleship Ministries department of Eastern Board. This department presently has six programs. Voluntary Service (VS), in operation for nearly forty years, continues to spark new commitment for involvement in the church, to nudge persons toward further education, and to help congregations focus on mission beyond themselves. About 55 persons serve under Voluntary Service each year.

A second program of Discipleship Ministries, Youth Evangelism Service (YES), offers three months of intensive discipleship training followed by four to seven months of cross-cultural mission assignments. Teams have served in Latin America, North America, Europe, Australia, Africa, and Asia. Its focus is on preparing young adults for evangelism and church building.

Summer Training Action Teams (STAT) is an eight-week program geared primarily to high school and college age youth who are interested in intensive Christian discipleship training and cross-cultural service. After four weeks of training, teams serve in Latin America, Europe, Africa, or the United States.

A fourth program under Discipleship Ministries, School of Witness (SOW), is designed for persons with previous Discipleship Ministries involvement or church leadership experience. Its purpose is to equip participants with the spiritual foundations, knowledge, and tools for application so they can more confidently carry out effective evangelism and mission. The program includes three months of intensive training followed by a minimum six-month internship in a church or ministry setting.

Millersville International House (MIH) is a residential ministry to international students which involves young adults and others in providing lodging, support services, tutoring, and a witness to Christ for international students at Millersville University and surrounding colleges.

The sixth program, Second Mile Ministries, offers service opportunities for volunteers ranging in length from one or two days to several months. This involves many retired persons, youth groups, and others who want to volunteer time and effort to serve the church are involved.

Lancaster Mennonites also do relief work. They respond to disasters such as tornadoes, floods, and hurricanes, often through home and overseas mission workers on location. In places where no mission exists, the response is often through Mennonite Disaster Service (MDS) or in cooperation with Mennonite Central Committee (MCC), whose international headquarters is located at Akron, Pennsylvania.

Eastern Board's annual budget in 1992 was $6.7 million, divided among overseas, home, youth, and relief ministries.

For the occasion of the Eastern Board's fiftieth anniversary, Paul Kraybill wrote:

> As we turn from the past to the future, we face a vastly different world. During these fifty years something has happened, not only to the world but also to us. There has been the insistent evidence that Christ was building his church around the world. Sometimes that church did not take the form and shape that we had expected. But there it was, not to be disregarded or underestimated—the living church of Christ Jesus in more places than we had dreamed of.

In *God's Call to Mission,* adopted March 1991, Eastern Board gives this "Mission Statement" reflecting its current outlook in missions:

> Eastern Mennonite Board of Missions and Charities is commissioned by Lancaster Mennonite Conference to cultivate a vision for world mission.
>
> We serve as a channel for congregations to fulfill corporately the biblical mandate for reconciliation and wholeness of all people in Christ Jesus.
>
> We proclaim by word and deed that Jesus Christ is the only Savior and Lord.
>
> We invite people, especially those who haven't had opportunity to respond to the good news, to receive the gift of salvation and the empowering of the Holy Spirit.
>
> We desire that these new believers also become caring communities in mission under the rule of Christ.
>
> We partner with others near and far to carry out ministries of compassion and evangelism, plant churches, equip disciples, train leaders, work for peace and justice, and cultivate fellowship.

Not all evangelism and mission activities have direct root in the Board's program. The women of the Lancaster Conference have their own branch of the churchwide organization, Women's Missionary and Service Commission (WMSC), which aims to include all women of the church in their varying services and spiritual gifts. Inspirational meetings are held annually. In addition, members of each congregation are free to involve themselves in other types of witness as they find opportunity. Community home Bible studies, summer Bible schools, sewing circles, crusades, seminars, and various meetings all are significant. It is the desire of the church that each person be a witness for Christ every day at work, at home, or wherever one finds oneself.

The Mennonite and Amish churches are not without problems. The increased affluence in the last several decades tends to weaken the witness of the church. Members get caught up in the materialistic aspects of life whether they live in the country or in the city, just as their neighbors do. Mennonites and Amish must constantly resist these pressures if they are to survive and maintain their historic perspective in an affluent society.

Glossary of Terms

ANABAPTIST—Literally "rebaptizer"; the name given by their enemies to the people who called themselves Swiss Brethren. The Amish, Mennonites, and Hutterites are direct descendants of the Anabaptists.

ASSURANCE OF SALVATION—Knowing that one is saved. In the past some thought it presumptuous to express this assurance. Some sects, including many of the Amish, continue to think that way. Mennonites today believe members can know that they have peace with God and will go to heaven.

BACKSLIDER—One who has been a member of the church, but who has become disobedient to the church.

BAN—The term used for the disciplinary action in which members will not eat or transact business with the member who is under a six-week probation until that member confesses the transgression and is reinstated, or does not submit and is excommunicated from the church and shunned indefintely.

BAPTISM—A religious rite symbolizing repentance from sin, accepting Christ as Savior and Lord, and the outpouring of the Holy Spirit. Pouring is the mode generally practiced by Amish and Mennonites.

BARN RAISING—The construction of a building by hundreds of volunteer workers. A large part of the project is completed on an appointed day. Women prepare a meal for the large working crew.

BEACHY AMISH—Also called Amish Mennonites, or Weavertown. A people more conservative than Mennonites, but allowing cars, electricity, telephones, and tractors. They do not shun members who leave to join less-plain churches.

BISHOP—An ordained overseer in Amish or Mennonite churches. He is responsible for the spiritual welfare of the members of the district or districts in his charge. The bishop is also responsible for the leadership over the ministers and deacons. He is chosen by lot from among the ministers or by other agreed-upon procedure.

BRETHREN—The name preferred by the early Anabaptists. They were also called the Swiss Brethren. Also used today for a denomination named Church of the Brethren.

COMFORTERS—Bedspreads that are soft, lightweight, but thick and warm; usually homemade.

COMMITMENT—Giving oneself to a cause. In this book, turning life over to the lordship of Christ and promising loyalty to him.

COMMUNION—An ordinance of the church. Members eat a small piece of bread and take a sip of wine or grape juice. These emblems represent the broken body and shed blood of Christ.

CONFESSION OF FAITH—An expression of belief. Refers to a decision made by a responsible adult or youth (not a child) to accept Christ as Savior and Lord. Upon this confession, one is entitled to baptism. This term also refers to the articles of faith stating the doctrinal position of a church.

CONSCIENTIOUS OBJECTOR or CO—One who for conscience' sake will not participate in military endeavor.

CONVERSION—An experience when one recognizes and admits one's sinful condition and accepts the forgiveness and new life made possible by the sacrificial death of Christ.

DEACON—An ordained official in the church who ministers to the material needs of the members and also provides counsel for church discipline. A deacon may read Scripture from the pulpit, make announcements, and preach in the absence of a minister, or as arranged by the ministerial team.

DISTRICT—A unit in the church organization. For Amish, a geographical area encompassing about thirty-five families. A Mennonite district includes a half dozen, more or less, congregations—usually in close proximity but in some cases scattered rather widely.

EXCOMMUNICATION—A disciplinary action when leaders refuse a

member the privileges and fellowship of church membership. This results when a member refuses to obey at some point either the doctrine or discipline of the church.

FOOT WASHING—The literal observance of Christ's command in John 13:4-17. Basins of water and towels are placed in the church or home where members pair off and wash each other's feet following the communion service.

INFANT BAPTISM—Practice of baptizing infant children. A point of difference between Anabaptists and the early churches during the Reformation. Anabaptists rebaptized, not recognizing baptism administered to an innocent child.

LOT—A method for choosing bishops, ministers, and deacons. Those nominated each select a hymnal, one of which contains the ordination slip.

MARTYRS—Those who died at the hands of persecutors rather than relinquish their religious faith.

MENNONITE CENTRAL COMMITTEE (MCC)—An agency with headquarters at Akron, Pennsylvania, which coordinates relief and service ministries for North American Mennonite and Brethren in Christ churches.

MENNONITE CHURCH—A general name which applies to the largest body of Mennonites in America and distinguishes them from sister groups such as the General Conference Mennonites. Lancaster Conference is part of the Mennonite Church.

MENNONITE DISASTER SERVICE (MDS)—An organization with headquarters at Akron, Pennsylvania, which mobilizes units of volunteers to aid victims of disaster caused by storm, flood, fire, earthquake, and so on.

MINISTER—An ordained leader charged with the responsibility of preaching and pastoring a congregation of the church. He is usually chosen by lot from among the membership.

NONRESISTANCE—A position against war and violence based on New Testament teaching.

OLD ORDER AMISH—The name of the largest body of Amish in America. The "Old Order" part of the name comes as a result of some groups departing from the main body in various details; only since coming to America are they called "Old Order."

OLD ORDER MENNONITES—Refers specifically to the Horning and Wenger Mennonites, officially the Weaverland and Groffdale conferences respectively. These people have also been known as Wisler or Martinites in the past.

ORDINATION—The service which includes laying on of hands when a bishop, minister, or deacon is installed as an official in the Mennonite or Amish Church.

PACIFISM—Opposition to war on a moral or humanistic basis.

PENNSYLVANIA DUTCH—A term broadly used to describe the German culture, customs, and dialect—more correctly Pennsylvania German. It has no connection with Holland Dutch. "Dutch" is a misnomer from the German word "Deutsch."

PERIOD OF INSTRUCTION—A series of classes where church officials teach applicants the doctrine and discipline of the church before they receive baptism.

PLAIN GARB—A distinctive way of dress; very modest, usually identifying the wearer with a certain religious group.

PRAYER VEILING—Also head covering, prayer cap, or devotional covering; worn by women in obedience to the scriptural teaching in 1 Corinthians 11.

PUBLISHED—When an Amish couple decides to marry, the intentions are announced, or "published," on a Sunday morning at preaching service prior to the wedding.

QUILTS—Homemade bed covers with fine stitchery over patchwork. The top often carries an intricate design made by sewing together small pieces of colorful fabric. A lining and fabric back complete the warm, practical, but attractive cover.

REFORMATION—A sixteenth-century religious awakening when the

Protestant churches began. During this time the Anabaptist movement also emerged.

REPENTANCE—Turning from sin to God, showing true sorrow and a desire to change.

SHUNNING—Refusing to eat or transact business with one who has been excommunicated from the church.

STATE CHURCH—Existing church structure at the time of the Anabaptist beginnings. A church had jurisdiction in a certain locality and legally required all babies born there to be baptized into that particular church. Anabaptists rejected this in favor of a believers church, holding to the separation of church and state.

SUNDAY SCHOOLS—Bible classes in the church or home, usually preceding the preaching service on Sunday morning.

SWISS BRETHREN—The early Anabaptists called themselves Brethren or Swiss Brethren.

VOCATIONAL SCHOOL—The three-hour session on Saturday which permits Amish youth to continue schooling the required years beyond the eighth grade while receiving most of their education through agricultural and domestic experience at home. This is in place of public high school for those who finish eighth grade before they are old enough to quit school.

VOLUNTARY BELIEVERS—A term used by the early Anabaptists to indicate that members joined by choice. This was in contrast to the state church practice.

VOLUNTARY SERVICE (VS)—An organized program to enable persons to engage in various service projects with minimum support.

WORLD—That portion of society which is viewed as unconverted and unchristian, together with its values, standards, goals, and attitudes. Mennonites and Amish are much concerned not to allow this "world" to lead them away from the pure and wholesome standards of New Testament Christianity.

Bibliography

(Unless otherwise noted, books are from Scottdale, Pa.: Herald Press.)

Amish Women, Committee of. *Amish Cooking*. Deluxe ed., 1980.

Augsburger, Myron A. *I'll See You Again!* 1989.

Braght, Thieleman J. van. *The Bloody Theater: Martyrs Mirror of the Defenseless Christians*. Compiled from various authentic chronicles, memorials, and testimonies. Tr. from the original Dutch ed. of 1660 by Joseph F. Sohm. Reprints of 3d English ed., 1938, 1992.

Dyck, Cornelius J., ed. *An Introduction to Mennonite History: A Popular History of the Anabaptists and Mennonites*. 3d ed., 1993.

Fisher, Sara E., and Rachel K. Stahl. *The Amish School*. Intercourse, Pa.: Good Books, 1986.

Gibbons, Phebe H. *Pennsylvania Dutch*. New York: AMS, Natural History Press, rev. ed., reprint of 1882 ed.

Good, Merle. *These People Mine*. 1973.

Good, Merle and Phyllis. *20 Most Asked Questions About the Amish and Mennonites*. Intercourse, Pa.: Good Books, 1979.

Hershey, Hiram, producer. *The Amish: A People of Preservation*. Video, 54-minute PBS Documentary, rev. 1991. Produced by Heritage Productions, Harleysville, Pa.

Horsch, James E., ed. *Mennonite Yearbook and Directory*, 1992, vol. 80. Scottdale, Pa.: Mennonite Publishing House, 1992.

Hostetler, John A. *Amish Life*. 1986.

_____. *Amish Society*. Baltimore: Johns Hopkins Press, 3d ed., rev., 1980.

_____. *Hutterite Life*. 1983.

_____. *Mennonite Life*. 1983.

Hostetler, John A., and Gertrude E. Huntington. *Children in Amish Society: Socialization and Community Education*. New York: Holt, Rinehart and Winston, Inc., 1971.

Kauffman, J. Howard, and Leo Driedger. *The Mennonite Mosaic: Identity and Modernization*. 1991.

Kollmorgen, Walter M. *Culture of a Contemporary Rural Community: The Old Order Amish of Lancaster County, Pennsylvania*. Rural Life Studies, vol. 4. U.S. Department of Agriculture, Bureau of Agricultural Economics, September 1942.

Kraybill, Donald B. *The Puzzles of Amish Life*. Intercourse, Pa.: Good Books, 1990.

_____. *The Riddle of Amish Culture.* Baltimore: The John Hopkins University Press, 1989.

Längin, Bernd G. *Die Amischen: Vom Geheimnis des einfachen Lebens.* Paul List Verlag in der Südwest Verlag GmbH & Co. KG, 1990. English tr., Herald Press, 1993.

Luthy, David. *Amish Settlements Across America.* Route 4, Aylmer, Ont.: Pathway Publishers, 1985.

MacMaster, Richard K. *Land, Piety, Peoplehood: The Establishment of Mennonite Communities in America, 1683-1790.* 1985.

Mennonite Confession of Faith. Adopted by Mennonite General Conference, August 22, 1963. 1963.

Mennonite Encyclopedia: A Comprehensive Reference Work on the Anabaptist-Mennonite Movement. Vols. 1-4, 1955-59; vol. 5, 1990.

Oyer, John S., and Robert S. Kreider. *Mirror of the Martyrs.* Intercourse, Pa.: Good Books, 1990.

Raber, Ben J. *The New American Almanac for 1992.* Baltic, Ohio: Raber's Book Store, 1992.

Scott, Stephen. *Amish Wedding and Other Special Occasions, The.* Intercourse, Pa.: Good Books, 1988.

_____. *Plain Buggies: Amish, Mennonite, and Brethren Horse-Drawn Transportation.* Intercourse, Pa.: Good Books, 1981.

_____. *Why Do They Dress That Way.* Intercourse, Pa.: Good Books, 1986.

Scott, Stephen, and Kenneth Pellman. *Living Without Electricity.* Intercourse, Pa.: Good Books, 1990.

Seitz, Ruth Hoover, and Blair Seitz. *Amish Ways.* Harrisburg, Pa.: R B Books, Seitz & Seitz, 1991.

Showalter, Mary Emma. *Mennonite Community Cookbook: Favorite Family Recipes.* 1950, 1978.

Spotts, Charles D., ed. *Denominations Originating in Lancaster County, Pennsylvania: Community Historians Annual,* no. 2. Lancaster, Pa.: Franklin and Marshall College Library, Dec. 1963.

Stahl, Martha Denlinger, *By Birth or By Choice: Who Can Become a Mennonite?* 1987.

Stoltzfus, Grant M. *Mennonites of the Ohio and Eastern Conference: From the Colonial Period in Pennsylvania to 1968.* 1969.

Verduin, Leonard. *The Reformers and Their Stepchildren.* Grand Rapids: William B. Eerdmans Publishing Co., 1964.

Wenger, J. C. *How Mennonites Came to Be. What Mennonites Believe. The Way to a New Life. The Way of Peace. Disciples of Jesus. A Faith to Live By.* Booklets in the Mennonite Faith Series, briefly describing major emphases of the New Testament as understood in the Anabaptist-Mennonite tradition.

Yoder, Joseph W. *Rosanna of the Amish.* 1973.

Yoder, Marvin K. *What We Believe About Children.* 1984.

Yoder, Paton, *Tradition and Transition.* 1990.

Index

Institutions, 79-84
Insurance, 60-62

Labor unions, 55
Lancaster Conference Mennonites, 14-15, 79-84
Language , 25, 35-37, 71
Lot, 37-40
Luther, Martin, 66
Lutheran, 71

Manz, Felix, 66-69
Marriage, 42-45
Medicine, 23
Mennonite Central Committee, 62-64, 82
Mennonite Disaster Service, 62-64, 82
Mennonite Information Center, 19
Mennonite Mutual Aid, 62
Mennonite Mutual Fire Insurance Assoc., 62
Mennonites
  historical origin, 66-70
  number of, 14-15
  origin of name, 67, 70
  to America, 71
  to Lancaster, 71
Moravian (Brethren), 71, 76
Mormons, 76

New Amish, 73
Newspapers, 22-23
Nonconformity, 21-25, 55. *See also* Dress
Nonresistance, 63-65, 68

Occupations, 53-59
Old Order Mennonites, 74
Old Order River Brethren, 75
Ordination, 37-40
Overseas missions, 79-84

Palatinate, 71
Penn, William, 71
Pennsylvania, 66, 71

Pennsylvania Dutch, 25, 36, 71
Persecution, 68-71
Picture taking, 16-18
Pikers, 74
Protestants, 66-69

Quakers, 76

Radio, 22
Reformation, 66-70
Reformed, 71
Reformed Mennonites (or New Mennonites), 74
Reidenbach Mennonites, 74
Reist, Hans, 70

Sattler, Michael, 69
Schleitheim, 69
Schwenkfelder, 71
Seventh-Day Baptists, 71, 76
Shunning, 44, 70
Simons, Menno, 67, 69-70
Singing, 35-37, 43-47
Social Security, 58
State church, 66-68
Statistics, 14-15, 50-51, 56
Sunday school, 37

Taxes, 19, 58, 65
Television, 22
Tobacco, 56
Tourism, 16-20

Voluntary Service, 81-82

Wealth, 56-58
Weddings, 42-45
Wenger Mennonites, 74
Worship service
  Amish, 35-37
  Mennonite, 37

Youth, 25-26

Zurich, 66-67
Zwingli, 66

The Author

One of five children in a Mennonite family, Martha Denlinger Stahl spent most of her growing-up years in a small rural town east of Lancaster. An Amish farm bordered the Denlinger property. So naturally the families became friends.

Martha taught school for twenty years in the Pequea Valley School District. She received her bachelor of science degree from Eastern Mennonite College, Harrisonburg, Virginia. At Millersville (Pa.) State College, she completed her master of education studies and took additional schooling leading to certification in elementary school counseling. In 1987 Herald Press published her second book, *By Birth or By Choice: Who Can Become a Mennonite?*

Martha and her husband, Omar B. Stahl, retained their home in Lancaster while serving in 1988-92 with Mennonite Home Missions in Bavaria, Germany, where Martha continued writing. She also enjoys travel, reading, needlecraft, and providing hospitality.

Lancaster County

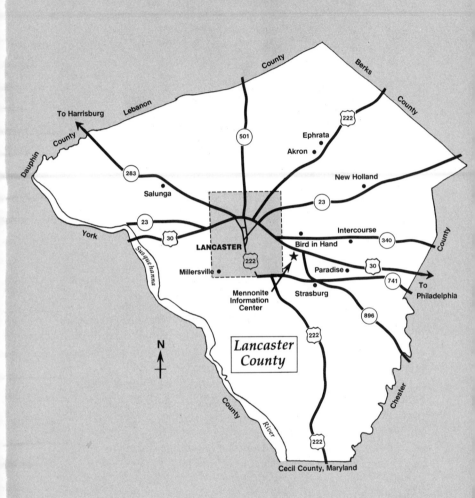